ISLAM
AS IT IS

Maulana Wahiduddin Khan

www.goodwordbooks.com

First published 1992
© Goodword Books 2005
Eighth reprint 2005

Translated by Farida Khanam

Goodword Books Pvt. Ltd.
1, Nizamuddin West Market
New Delhi 110 013
e-mail: info@goodwordbooks.com

Printed in India

www.goodwordbooks.com

Contents

Foreword

Life and the Universe pose certain questions to the thinking individual, and how he answers them depends largely on his pattern of thinking. What, in the first place, establishes this pattern? It is quite simply, the urge to worship. But to worship whom, or what?

A man either worships God, or some entity other than God. His whole way of thinking is then governed by his choice. All his trust and devotion are centred in that Being or thing: that is what becomes the most important force in his life, for his actions flow from his faith and his urge to worship. That, in effect, is what makes up his religion.

Islam, the preserved form of religion, teaches us that behind this world, the will of an all-powerful Creator and Master is at work. One day, everyone will be brought before Him to be judged, and on that fateful day, His will be the final word on human success or failure.

The discovery of this Reality is of much greater importance than the discovery of a mere mathematical formula. It is to recognise that one is nothing, has nothing, that God is everything , has everything in His power, is Lord of all creation. With this realization comes the desire to become a slave of the Almighty. One who makes this discovery becomes, quite naturally, a completely altered human being, for his life is then bathed in a divine light; his heart and mind are completely captivated. When he hears and sees, it is with the hearing and vision of his Maker. The darkness in which his ideas and thinking had formerly been plunged, is banished by the discovery of God; every fibre of his being is lit up by this discovery, just as if a new sun had climbed into the sky.

The discovery of God takes place in the human mind, but a man feels its effect throughout his entire being. He loses himself and finds God. With God living in his thoughts he belongs entirely to Him. His entire being is enslaved and prostrates itself before his Lord. One excellent consequence of this is his beginning to treat his fellow human beings as befits a devout servant of God. Where others act out of egoism, he proceeds with humility. Where others are vengeful in attitude, he is invariably forgiving. Where others are cruel and unjust, he is always kind and merciful. Where people, thinking only of themselves cut themselves off from others, he comes closer to people in order to keep up good social relations. Whereas others prefer to keep what they have in order to increase their own prosperity, he derives pleasure from giving to others. While people chase after the pleasures of this world, he remains absorbed in the hidden world of the Hereafter. Such is the life of truth which has been shown in all its perfection through the teachings and examples of the Prophet.

To follow their example is to attach oneself to God. Those who do so also attach themselves, quite naturally, to their fellow-men, wishing, as they do, to share with them the goodness they have found. Their outward conduct thus begins to reflect their inner state.

It is natural that, in this world, everyone should live for some thing. Some live for money, some for power, some for glory. There is no one who does not have some cherished desire, the attainment of which gives him a major satisfaction in life. The objects of human ambition are numberless, and can arouse in the human breast all kinds of hopes, fears, longings and agonies. The fulfilment of these ambitions is obviously associated with happiness, and their non-fulfilment with grief.

Religion directs human beings just as certainly towards

a goal, but it is along quite another path, because the goal, itself, is so different. The kind of life led by those directed in this way entirely depends upon the nature of the religion they have adopted. Their thinking, emotions, activities, commitments, transactions all revolve around whatever has been accepted by them as their religion. Their lives are ruled by it, so that just as they make all-out efforts in their everyday lives to attain material goals, so do they spare no effort to attain the non-material goals placed before them by religion. Even if they cannot draw near to these goals, they take care to do nothing which would take them further away from them.

The non-material goal of religion demands the same will, effort, concentration and dedication as the material goal. But the quality of such application in the former case is superior, because it is illuminated by divine inspiration, whereas in the latter case it definitely is not. Waking or sleeping, the devotee clings to his religion throughout his entire life as the mainstay of his existence. There is no particle of his being which remains insensitive to the effects of religion.

Religion, as viewed by individuals of differing beliefs, may pertain to God, or may pertain to entities other than God. Everyone is free to adopt whichever religion he pleases. But free as he is, it is in his choice of religion that man is being put to the test in this world. His choice of a God-centred, or a godless religion will be what determines his fate in the life after death. Men are led astray by the fact that it is quite possible to choose a godless religion, and yet be materially successful in this world; one may ignore God, and yet have honour and glory in this life. What they do not see is that none of this means anything at all in the life after death. Worldly successes accompany one only as far as the grave. Beyond the grave, a man who has depended solely on material things to support him through life, will find himself at that point totally bereft of any props on which he could conceivably lean. He will come face to face with the Almighty, in all His Power and Glory, and thanks to his godless religion, he will find himself utterly defenceless. The only man to have honour and success in the Heareafter will be one who has taken God's religion to himself while still in the land of the living. Beyond the grave, it is too late; he who has adopted a godless religion will be faced with eternal doom in the afterlife.

The religion of God is the true, natural religion to adopt. The truth of this suddenly becomes plain in moments of crisis. Whatever the religion a man adopts, when the whirlpool of events sends him spiralling downwards to his doom, he forgets all else and turns to God. It is experiences of this nature which prove that the only true religion is the religion of God, the one on which a man should base his entire life. If he adopts any other religion, a time will come, sooner or later when it will prove to be without substance. When disaster looms large, all its supports will be shown to be false.

Nature provides a pointer towards the future, everlasting world. One who listens to its appeal, and moulds his life accordingly, will be the truly successful individual in this life, and in the Hereafter.

1

Man, Know Thyself!

If scientists were one day to declare that the earth's gravity had been reduced to zero, and that our planet was being pulled towards the sun at 6,000 m.p.h, the whole world would be stricken with panic, for this would mean that in a few weeks time all life would be burnt off the face of the earth.

This globe, in fact, is always in much greater peril even than this. But no one loses a moment's sleep over it. What, actually, is this peril? It is the peril of the Last Day, to which the world from the moment of creation has been destined, and towards which we are rushing in the most reckless way. As a matter of faith, most of us accept this reality, but, strangely, we do not stop to give it any serious consideration.

If different people were asked what was the topic of the greatest relevance for mankind today, they would all give different answers. Some would say the spread of nuclear weapons, some would say too high a birthrate all over the world, while others might say that the most important of all was the production of wealth and the giving of fair shares to all. These widely differing opinions show that people in general do not properly recognize what they themselves are. If they did, they would all argue that what affects man most is his ignorance of his own nature, and his refusal to accept the fact that one day he must die, and, more terrible, be called to account before his Maker. If we could only accept this reality, we would think less of the present world and more of the afterlife.

Today, most people do believe in God and in the afterworld. It is not as if they deny these things; yet their actions do not conform to their beliefs. In practice, all people are concerned about is getting on in life.

If you stand in a busy shopping centre during the evening rush-hour you will soon become aware of what it is that people are rushing towards; they are rushing towards the satisfaction of their own desires. One need only look at them, and listen to them, to understand that buying and selling, acquiring objects or money, are what give them the greatest joy in life. The happiness or sadness we see in their faces are directly connected with success or failure in the fulfillment of material ambitions. No one cares about tomorrow. Everyone wants his share of the good things of life right this minute, and even being accepted and liked by other people would appear to depend on the type and amount of one's possessions.

Everyone, in fact, wants the world. No one wants the afterworld. No one, indeed, even thinks about it. And this state of affairs is to be found not only in our big cities, but even in the tiniest of villages. Wherever one goes, people have the same obsessions. Male and female, rich and poor, young and old, townsman and countryman, religious or irreligious — all are running in this same direction. All are frittering away their precious time and talents on material gain. What an obsession! No sacrifice, however dubious in character, is too great if it brings them such things. Even faith and conscience are sacrificed at the alter of worldly gain. No compromise is too base.

Success of this kind, however, is trivial and without meaning, for it will be of no avail in the after-life. One who assures his worldly position at the cost of his after-life is like the man who does not care to save up for his old age while he is still young. Eventually a time comes when his limbs fail him and he can no longer work for a living. It is only then that he realizes his predicament: he is without food, clothes or shelter, and he can no longer provide for himself. How many have we seen lying in rags, in the shade of some wall, with dogs barking and snapping around them, and boys throwing stones at them. We have seen many such pitiable sights, but we are not so shaken by what we see that we feel the need to take any precautions. None of us actually see ourselves coming to such an end, because we are too concerned with the present. Who cares for tomorrow?

When, in wartime, the air-raid siren announces the approach of squadrons of enemy bombers coming to blast us to eternity, we are chilled by this idea, and everyone immediately dashes to the air-raid shelters. In a matter of moments, the streets are deserted. Anyone who does not react to the alert in this way is considered idiotic, if not mentally deranged. But what happens when men of religion sound the Lord's alert ? "Mankind! Worship Me. Fulfill your obligations to one another and live in accordance with My will. I will punish those who fail to do this in a way that cannot be imagined. They will writhe forever in a torment from which they will never be able to free themselves." What happens, indeed? Everyone has heard this warning, but no one acknowledges its force, its authority, its essential truth. The general attitude is to treat it as a matter of no consequence, to be thought about later, or perhaps not at all.

To gain worldly advantages, people do not stop at anything. In this way the caravan of life is hastening onwards to a point of no return. People start in response to the siren's wail, but ignore the warnings of the Lord of the Universe. Far from hastening to do what is right at the very sound of it, no one even alters his pace.

What is the reason for this very strange state of affairs? It is simply that the siren warns us of the dangers of this world, the consequences of which will immediately be felt, whereas the danger signals given by the Lord relate to the after-life, which is very far ahead (so we think!) in the future. Between us and these perils there stands the wall of death, which no human eye can penetrate.

We do not see behind it the engulfing smoke and fire of Hades. Although people respond immediately to the air raid siren, they remain unaffected by divine warnings of calamity. The absolute certainty of their doom has no immediacy and, this being so, they do not feel any urge to begin leading righteous lives to atone for their sins.

God Almighty, however, has given us not only our two eyes with which to perceive the external world, but also a 'third eye' with which to scan the invisible realities beyond the normal limits of human perception. This third eye is the intellect. People remain in a state of doubt and ignorance, because they do not care to use this 'third eye.' They reckon that the total reality is what they can see with their own two eyes. If they were just to give the matter some earnest thought, they would become even more certain about what remains unseen than about what is visible.

What is the one reality that everyone has to acknowledge? The obvious and unanimous answer to this is death. Death is a reality to which everyone, big or small, great or humble, has to reconcile himself. Everyone realizes that death can overtake one at any moment, but whenever this thought takes shape, people think only of what will happen to their children after they die, and what domestic and financial arrangements they should make for them. So much of their time is spent in safeguarding their children's interests in this life, that they make no efforts to ensure themselves for the life beyond the grave. They do not appear able to project their minds beyond the point of death. They behave as if only their children will survive them; as if they themselves will be non-existent and will, therefore, have nothing to prepare for.

People behave as if they are totally unaware of the fact

that there is a life after death, whereas, in fact, the real life only commences after death. If they could only realize that when they enter the grave, it is not just to be buried, but to be ushered into another world, their concern would be more for their own fate than for their children's future. Even those who expect to find a life after death more consequential than the present one, do little to prepare themselves for it. This goes both for the religious-minded and the agnostics.

There are two factors which arouse doubts about life after death. Firstly, on dying, all human beings turn into dust, and all traces of their bodies eventually disappear. Once this has happened, how can they possibly be revived? Secondly, we cannot actually see the life after death. And if no one has ever seen it, how can we be certain that it exists? How can we know that when we die, that life will be there for us to step into? Let us look at both these objections in turn.

Life After Death.

"When I am dead, will I then be raised up again?" This question may arise in a vague kind of way in the minds of even those who do not have any strong beliefs in life after death as a reality. But the fact remains that very few people give their direct attention to this question. The plain fact that tomorrow's life is not the subject of eager and willing enquiry is surely a sign that people have conscious or subconscious doubts as to its existence.

If, however, we give serious thought to this reality, it ceases to be difficult to understand. God—wishing to put us to the test—has not told us the secrets of life after death. But He has scattered His signs throughout the world, and it is then for us to mark them, think earnestly about them, and in this way find a true picture of the essence of all things. This universe is, indeed, a mirror in which we can gaze upon the image of the next world.

15

It is well known that human beings pass from a prior state to their present state. Man takes shape from a substance which, itself formless, grows inside the mother's womb until a fully-fledged human being develops, ready to enter the outside world. This process of change, which turns an invisible, unfeeling, valueless substance into a six-foot tall human being, is an every day event, so why should there be any difficulty in understanding how the tiny particles of our bodies, after being scattered in the ground, will once again take on a human form?

Every individual that one sees walking around is, in fact, an accumulation of countless atoms which had previously been dispersed throughout the earth and atmosphere in unknown dimensions. These atoms, brought together to form one meaningful, sensate pattern, then took the shape of a human being capable of thought, feeling and movement. The same process will be repeated in reverse order when we die. The particles which had made up our body will be diffused in the earth, the water, the air, and later, at God's command, they will be reassembled and again take the shape of a human being. What is so extraordinary about a happening which so constantly repeats itself?

Even in the world of matter, there are clear signs of the revival of life. Every year, in the rainy season, vegetation flourishes and greenery spreads in all directions. But when this season is over, the sun dries everything up. It is as if it had passed the death sentence on all seasonally growing things. A plain where flowers had formerly bloomed now seems a barren waste. But when the rains come again, that very same vegetation will be revived by the water pouring down from the heavens, and the dried-up plain will again become a meadow. In this very same way, man will be brought back to life after his death.

Let's look at the matter from another angle. If doubts occur concerning life after death, it is because what we imagine is based on what happens in our present physical existence. We consider the solid, moving body that we can see to be the essential human being, and wonder how something which takes this shape can be re-made and raised up again once it has rotted away and mingled with the earth. We observe that when death strikes, the once articulate human being falls forever silent, the once mobile human being comes to a standstill. In fact, all his faculties cease to function. Shortly afterwards, he is buried, cremated or thrown into a river depending upon the customs of the people concerned. A few days later, the body is reduced to tiny particles and mingles with the earth or water in such a way as to be no longer detectable by normal human vision. We witness this process every so often, yet find it hard to understand how once alive human beings, who now have no physical substance to them, can be revived in any manner whatsoever.

What we fail to appreciate is that the word 'man' refers not to any such bodily form, but rather to the soul which inhabits the body. As far as the physical frame is concerned, we know that it is made up of tiny units called living cells. The position of the cells in our bodies is like that of the bricks in a building. The bricks (or cells) of our bodies, are continuously being destroyed in the course of our daily lives and we compensate for this loss by taking in food. This food, once digested, produces a variety of different types of cells which make up for any physical deficiency. The human body is thus undergoing a constant process of erosion and change. Old cells are destroyed and new ones take their place. This process continues daily, until finally, a total renewal of the body is complete, usually within a ten-year period. To put it in another way, nothing whatsoever now remains of the body you possessed ten years ago. Your present physique is an entirely new one. If all the parts of your body which were discarded over the last ten years were to be gathered together again, another human being exactly resembling yourself could be put together. If you are a hundred years old, then ten "you's " could be formed. But even if they looked exactly like you, they would just be lifeless lumps of flesh, for "you" do not dwell in them. "You" have cast off these old bodies and moulded yourself into a new frame.

So the drama of construction and destruction is constantly being enacted within you, without there being any apparent change in you. The entity which you call 'yourself' remains as it has always been. Supposing you had entered into a contract with someone ten years ago, "You" would continue to honour this contract, because "You" had committed yourself to it, although your previous frame is now non-existent. The hands which signed the contract and the tongue which testified to it are no longer parts of your body. Nevertheless, "You" still exist, and "You" acknowledge the fact that this ten-year old agreement was contracted by "You" and that "You" will continue to abide by it. This is that internal human being at work which, far from altering along with body-changes, survives countless transformations intact.

This proves that the expression, "homo sapiens," far from being a label attached to a certain physical form, which ceases to exist after death, in fact denotes a separate entity which remains intact even after the scattering of the different elements of the body. The fact that the body alters, whereas the soul does not, is conclusive proof of the transitional nature of the body and the eternal nature of the soul.

There is the view that life and death are the accumulation and subsequent diffusion of countless particles of matter. Those who hold this view, are, of course, misguided. It has been expressed thus by the Urdu poet Chakbast: *"Zindgi kya hai anaasir ka zuhoore tarteeb. Maut kya hai inhi ajza ka pareshan hona."* (What is life? Elements arranging themselves in order. And death? Their diffusion).

But this statement is simply not borne out by fact. If

life were simply "elements arranging themselves in order," then it ought to follow that so long as this order endured, life should continue to survive, and conversely, it should be possible for scientists to create life by causing elements to accumulate in a particular way. Quite obviously both these propositions are false.

Let us take the first proposition. Consider the corpse of a man who has died of heart failure. All its elements are still arranged in the same order as they were a few minutes beforehand, no significant changes having taken place. But those elements are now lifeless. The corpse is still an "orderly elemental manifestation." but the soul which once inhabited it has now departed. This shows that the organization of elemental matter neither creates nor sustains life. We all know that it is not just those who have been torn limb from limb in accidents who die. People of all ages and in all states of health regularly pass away, and it frequently happens that doctors cannot say— particularly in the case of strokes, heart failure, etc. — why a patient should have died at that particular point in time. It so often happens that a man is perfectly healthy one day and is dead the next. Life, we must concede, is a separate entity from the body.

As for the second proposition – the creation of a live human being in a laboratory— scientists are the first to admit that this is a sheer impossibility. They say this, although the body's chemical formula and atomic structure are well-known. Its carbon is the same as in charcoal, its oxygen and hydrogen the same as in water and its nitrogen the same as in the atmosphere. It has never been true to say that a live human being is just a specific collection of ordinary atoms which have been arranged in an extraordinary way. Man may be made up of certain known material particles, but we are still not in a position to create life by just combining those particles in a particular way. The body of a live human being is not just a collection of lifeless atoms. It is something quite other than this. It is a combination of atoms plus life. After death, this collection of atoms does not disappear from view. It is still there for everyone to see. It is life itself which departs for another world.

Clearly, life is not something which can be completely annihilated. Once we understand that it is something having eternal properties, we can appreciate how rational, and also how natural the 'life-after-death' theory is. Facts are simply crying out that life does not consist merely of what can be seen of the human body prior to death. There must also be a life after death. If the human intellect accepts the passing nature of this world, the possessor of that intellect must be a being who survives it. When we die, we do not pass into oblivion. We retire to reside in another world. The present world is nothing but the briefest of interludes in our never-ending life-span.

The Other World.

Think for a moment what this other world must be like. God's Prophet has made it known to mankind that heaven and hell both exist there, and that everyone who dies must eventually find his eternal abode   in one or the other. Those who are obedient to God in this world, always behaving in a virtuous fashion, will be rewarded with a place in paradise, while those who are evil and rebellious in their attitude towards God will be cast into the Fire to be tormented for ever and ever.

It is important to understand that human actions fall into one of two categories. The first comprises everyday, routine matters in which there is no need to label actions right or wrong. It also includes purely accidental happenings, which, likewise, cannot be labelled right or wrong, because of there being no human will or intention behind them. The second category, however, is very different in nature because it covers a wide range of actions, the rights and wrongs of which must be taken seriously into consideration before being carried out. This is known as the ethical category.

Imagine walking along a mountain road with ledges of rock projecting above your head. Suddenly a piece of rock detaches itself, falls on you and injures you. Do you strike the mountainside and bear a grudge against it? Of course not. The stone falling down and hurting you was purely a matter of chance. But suppose a man picks up a stone and throws it at you with the clear intention of injuring you. Won't you then become enraged and feel like throwing stones back at him? You would be quite right in feeling that he should be punished, because what he did was intentional. Here, it is not just a question of some accidental happening, but of right and wrong action, good and bad intentions, in a word— of ethics.

The examples chosen to clarify this point are of a very simple nature, in that the result of the action can immediately be seen, and, in the second case, one can judge immediately that the assailant was in the wrong. But, in life, there are much more complex situations where wrongdoing is not immediately apparent, and the culprits may go scot-free for long periods, or never be brought to book at all. Obviously, they should be condemned by their fellow-men or be punished by a court of law. But sometimes evil deeds are not seen to be such, or the wrong-doers are so clever as to escape punishment, or there simply may not be the means to inflict a suitable punishment. Crimes are often repeated for just such reasons. But the evil-doer should not be too ready to congratulate himself on the success of his schemes, or on his ability to evade the law— or the censure of society, for it is exactly this type of action that he will be called to account for by his Creator on the Day of Judgement. Everyone, no matter the walk of life he hails from, will be required to stand before his **Maker** on that fateful day, and lay bare his entire life before Him. Judged by those of his actions which fall into the ethical category,

21

where principles and right action are of supreme importance, he will either be ushered into paradise, or cast down into the flaming pits of hell. If all this has been kept hidden from him in this world, it is because it is God's intention to put man to the test.

It is in the afterworld that man will be faced with the full consequences of his deeds, depending upon how right or wrong they were. Every action has certain consequences for the doer; every situation that he creates causes a favourable or unfavourable reaction. In deciding upon the course he takes, for good or for evil, he himself forges his own destiny.

The Afterworld

At this point, the question arises as to the actual existence of the afterworld. In what way is it to be understood? In what way can it be made intelligible to us?

Let us take sound, which we cannot see and can only sometimes hear. It is the name for waves which form an invisible pattern in the air and which continue to exist thousands of years after the source of the sound is no longer in existence. In the case of the human voice, it is so indelibly imprinted upon the atmosphere that, if we possessed the apparatus to detect it, it could be replayed to us in its original form, and many would be the historic discussions upon which we could then eavesdrop. Just as we are enveloped by a blanket of air on which every word of ours is engraved, without our being able to see either the air or the 'inscription,' so the other world constantly envelopes us, recording our actions and our intentions. In this way they are imprinted there for all time, for the Almighty to read after we pass away.

Imagine a record, revolving in silence on a turntable. We place the needle in its groove, and, immediately, the room is filled with the sound of music. Not a single note is missed. None of its subtleties are lost. Similarly, the record of our lives will give forth every detail of our thoughts, words and deeds, not when a needle is placed in the groove, but when our Lord utters the word of command. The entire history of our lives, recorded right from the moment of birth, will thus be played back to us— whether to our joy or to our discomfiture will depend on the kind of lives we have led. On hearing this 'play-back,' people will ask," what sort of a book is this which has omitted neither the smallest nor the gravest of matters?" (Quran).

A Last Word

Just take a few minutes to think over everything I have explained. Consider that you are destined for an extremely long and unbroken lifespan. And make no mistake about the meaning of death. Death is by no means the end of this life. It marks the beginning of a new era. It is simply the dividing point between the two stages in our life. Think of the farmer who invests his capital in a crop, who sedulously cultivates it until it ripens, then harvests it and stores it for his year's requirements. Harvesting is the end of just one phase in the crop's development. Before that, it had been all toil and expense for the farmer. It is only after that point that he enjoys the fruits of his efforts. Such is the case with our life in this world too. Here we invest in and cultivate our after-world crop. Each one of us owns a field which is either cultivated or allowed to lie fallow. We use seeds which give us either a high or a low yield. After sowing our crop, we either attend to it properly or neglect it. We grow thorns or we grow fruit. We grow weeds or we grow flowers. Whatever we do, the period of our preparation of this crop lasts until the day we die. The day of our death is harvest day. That is the day that we shall reap as we have sown. When our eyes close on this world, they will open on the after-life and there, before our eyes, will be the crop which we have been busy cultivating (or neglecting) all our lives.

It is worth remembering that the person who does the farming is the one who does the harvesting, and that he will reap only the crop that he has sown. In the after-world, too, everyone will reap the harvest he had prepared for himself while he was still in the world of the living. Every farmer knows full well that he will take to the granary only as much grain as he has grown, and that the crop can never be other than what he had sowed.

In the afterworld, man's reward or punishment will be in direct proportion to the goodness or evil of his actions, to the goodness or evil of his intentions, and to the earnestness with which he courts good and shuns evil. Death puts a full stop to the period of his endeavours, and leads him to the final point at which he will experience their results. What a critical matter this is! If only man could come to a mature understanding of this before he died! Afterwards, his realization of this will be of no avail. It is too late to become aware of the truth after death for then there is no time to consider the gravity of one's errors, no time for repentance, no time for atonement.

Man's destiny is unknown to him. He is barely aware that time is conveying him at a breakneck pace towards the harvesting of his crop. While he considers himself occupied in a worthwhile way, all he may actually be doing is straining after paltry worldly profits; he may just be frittering away his precious time. He has before him a wonderful opportunity to ensure a sublime future for himself, but, more often than not, he chooses to waste his time on trivialities.

His Lord is calling him towards paradise, a place of eternal honour and bliss, while he, in his ignorance, is bent on pursuing pleasures which are illusory, and which cannot last. He reckons that he is adding to his happiness and prosperity, but, in actual fact, he is squandering whatever could be good about his life. He builds his worldly mansion, fondly imagining that he is building for his life, but, in fact, he is erecting walls of sand which will crumble away to nothing.

Man! Recognize yourself! Know what you are doing, and what you ought to be doing!

2

Belief in God

This world has one God. He is its Creator and Master. The greatest proof of God's existence is the existence of the world itself. Spread around us in all its vastness and complexity it bears witness to the existence of a great God who, in His infinite power, controls it. If we have no choice but to believe in the world, we have no choice but to believe in God as well, for the world would be meaningless if we did not accept the existence of a Maker and Master along with it. Look at how exquisitely the world has been fashioned. How can it be that it has no Maker? Look at the perfect or-·der which it maintains. Could it really be that no one is controlling it? The answer, of course, is that it could not. The truth is that, just as man is bound to believe in the world around him, so also is he bound to believe in God.

Suppose we ·placed a pebble on a potter's wheel, and then spun the wheel around very fast. The pebble would, of course, fly off, even although a potter's wheel can hardly reach a speed of 25 miles an hour. Now, just think for a moment that the earth we live on is also revolving but at a much faster rate than the potter's wheel. Yet we do not fly off. The earth spins continuously on its axis at a speed of 1000 miles an hour— much faster than the average passenger plane— yet we move around on its surface, and live our daily lives without any fear of being thrown off like the pebble from the potter's wheel. What a miracle this is. The explanation scientists give us is that the earth pulls us with great force from underneath, while the pressure of the atmosphere from above pushes us firmly to the ground. A force attracting us from below, and a five-hundred mile thick blanket of air enveloping us from above are miracles enough in themselves, and to say that they explain our not flying off into space is to lend even greater credence to the miraculous nature of our entire world.

Everything in this world, is, in fact, a miracle. Just think what happens when we put tiny seeds into the ground. The soil in which they are planted is uniform in constitution, but they bring forth a vast array of plants—radishes, carrots, turnips, guavas, mangoes, mustard plants— everything indeed from the humblest blade of grass to the mightiest oak. Each plant has its own distinct appearance, taste and fragrance, and, according to its species, gives certain benefits to mankind.

On all sides of us, a whole world of miraculous diversity and proportions stretches out before our eyes. Moreover, at every instant, a great variety of life forms are continually coming into existence, quite unaided by man. Yet if all of the human beings in this world were to come together, they would not be able to create even one tiny grain of sand. This all amounts to a miracle of such amazing proportions, that words fail us when we have to describe it. When we try to do so, we only degrade it, for we are unable to do justice to it with mere human words. All we can do is look on in wonder, and ask ourselves: "Besides God, who could have made manifest such a miracle?"

Everything in this world is made up of atoms. In its final analysis, every object is a collection of these tiny particles. Yet by some strange miracle, when these atoms come together in certain proportions, they form the dazzling globe of the sun, and when the same atoms accumulate elsewhere in different proportions they flow in cascades: in yet other places, they take the form of subtle breezes or are fashioned into fertile soil. All these things may be made up of the same atoms, but the nature and properties of each separate object are widely different.

This miraculous world provides man with endless resources which he puts to good use whenever he learns how to tap them. Massive supplies of whatever he needs in life are constantly being accumulated, and man himself has to do very little in order to avail of them. Take, for instance, the food that he eats. He has but to stretch out his hand for the huge quantities of valuable nourishment which, as part of the order of the cosmos, has been made available to him. Once he has it in his possession, all he has to move are his hands and his jaws so that the food should reach his stomach. Then without any further effort on his part, the food is absorbed by the body and is turned into flesh, blood, bones, nails, hair and other parts of the human body. Where food keeps the human body going, petroleum, another great earthly phenomenon, keeps his activities going. All man has to do is to extract it from the ground, refine it, put it into his machines and, astonishingly, this liquid fuel keeps the entire mechanism of his civilization running smoothly. Countless resources of this type have been created in this world, and there is enough of everything to meet man's needs. Man's part in bringing these things into being, or in changing them into some useful form, is a relatively small one. Therefore, with the minimum of effort, he has his clothes, houses, furniture, machines, vehicles and all the other components and accessories of his civilization. Are such occurrences not sufficient to prove that there is indeed a Maker and a Master of this world?

But we must not forget that there is another side to all this. Nature has provided us with a pure and beautiful world, yet what have our own actions made of it? We may have refined petroleum and made machines out of iron, but we have also filled the land and sea with corruption. We have converted the world into an arena of smoke, noise, pollution, vandalism and war. We have taken these things to such extremes that quite frequently there appears to be no solution to the man-made problems surrounding us. Very little has been accomplished in our factories, and indeed, in the whole field of technology. The world around us accomplishes much more than we human beings do. No problems are created by the works of nature, but man's work is constantly bedevilled by problems.

The earth rotates unceasingly in two ways— on its own axis and in orbit around the sun. But it does not create any noise in the process. A tree goes to work in the way of a great factory, but it does not emit any smoke. Daily, innumerable creatures are dying in the sea, but they do not pollute the water. The universe has been running in accordance with the divine order for billions of years, without ever having to reorganize itself, for everything about the way it is organized is so perfect. There are countless stars and planets moving around in space: they keep to the same speed, never lagging behind, and never exceeding their set pace. All these are miracles of the highest order. They are far more wonderful than anything that man can create, and they happen every instant in this world of ours. What further proof do we need that the power of a Great God lies behind this world?

When we look at the different life forms, we witness an astonishing spectacle. Certain material objects come together in one body, and there comes into being a creature like a fish swimming through water, or a bird soaring in the skies. Of the great variety of creatures which abound on the earth, the one of greatest interest to us is Man. In ways that are a mystery to us, he is moulded into a well-proportioned form. The bones within him take on the meaningful shape of the skeleton, which is covered with flesh and sealed in by a layer of skin, out of which sprout hair and nails. With blood coursing through channels within this frame, all of this adds up to a human being who walks about, holds things in his hands, who hears, smells, tastes, who has a mind which remembers things, accumulates information, analyses it and then expresses it in speech and in writing.

The formation of such an amazing being from inert matter is more than a miracle. The particles of which a man is composed are the same as that of earth and stone. But have we ever heard a piece of earth talking, or seen a piece of stone walking around? The word miraculous is barely adequate to describe the capabilities of man. But what else is there to this walking, talking, thinking, feeling man which distinguishes him from earth and stone? This factor— life— is still a mystery to us: there must indeed be a superior Being who has imbued inert matter with this quality, thus accomplishing a unique feat of creation.

Man has only to think of the nature of his own being to understand the nature of God. The self, the ego in man, has an individuality of its own, which is quite distinct from that of others of his kind living here on this earth. The ego in man is absolutely sure of its own existence. It is the part of man which thinks, feels, forms opinions, has intentions and puts them into practice. It also decides for itself which course of action to take. Every human being is thus a separate personality with a will and power of his own. Since our experience of such a being is an every day matter, what is astonishing about the existence of God, who also is a being wielding personal power, although on a scale far greater than ourselves? Believing in God is a very similar mental process to believing in one's own self. That is why the Quran says that man himself is ample evidence for himself, however much he may excuse himself (75: 14-15).

People demand some miraculous proof before they will believe in the truth of God and His message. But what further proof do they require when they have the miracle of the whole of the universe which has been functioning perfectly for millions of years on the vastest of scales? If the doubter is not prepared to accept such a great miracle, then how is he going to shed his doubts when he sees lesser miracles? In truth, man has been provided with everything he needs to enable him to believe in God, and then to place himself at His service. If, in spite of this, he does not believe in God, and fails to acknowledge God's power and perfection, then it is he himself and not anyone else who is to blame.

One who has found God has found everything. After the discovery of God, no further discovery remains to be made. Thus, when a man has discovered God, his entire attention is focussed upon Him. God, for him, becomes a treasure which he cherishes, and it is to Him then that he has recourse for all his worldly and eternal needs.

Suppose someone eats an apple, but detects no flavour in it and receives no nourishment from it. He might be said not to have eaten an apple at all, but only something which looks like an apple. The same is true of one's realization of God. A man who has truly discovered God will blissfully savour the essence of the experience. Anyone who claims to have discovered God without this accompanying sense of elation has certainly made no such discovery. He has only discovered something which he mistakenly thinks is God. He is like the man eating a fake apple and deriving no satisfaction from it.

God's world is a collection of atoms. In its elemental form, it all consists of one and the same type of inert matter; but God has moulded this matter into countless diverse forms : light, heat, greenery, flowing water. He has also invested lifeless matter with the properties of colour, taste and smell; and everywhere, he has set things in motion, having carefully controlled this motion by gravity. Discovering the God who has made such a world is much more than just acquiring a dry creed; it means filling one's heart and soul with the radiant glow of divine light and opening one's mind to incredible beauty and delicacy.

When we eat delicious fruits, this gives us a great sense

of enjoyment. When we hear beautiful music we are quite entranced by it. When a handsome child is born to a couple, their joy knows no bounds. Then what of our experience of God, who is the source of all beauty, joy and virtue? On discovering Him, can one remain unmoved? This is something which is hardly imaginable, for such a sublime experience— like coming close to a source of dazzling radiance— must surely leave its mark on one.

Having endowed things with their unique qualities, God Himself must have qualities that His discoverers may savour. To discover Him, therefore, is to experience Him like a fragrance in the nostrils, a taste which excites the palate, a texture which is a joy to caress, a melody which touches the heart. To come close to Him is to live in an everlasting garden of brilliant colours and delicate fragrances. It is to hear such music that one might wish its enchantment to last forever.

The Creator of all light, God Himself is the most resplendent of all beings. He is the light of the Heavens and of the earth, shedding His radiance on the personalities of all who discover Him. His is the greatest treasure house of all true wisdom. He is the greatest repository of all true strength. His discoverers are so fortified by His strength and so enlightened by His wisdom that no flood or hurricane can carry them away. They cannot, once having known Him, do other than evolve into superior human beings.

3

Prophethood

Certain non-Muslims once came before the Prophet Muhammad, upon whom be peace, and asked him for proof that he was a true prophet. They pointed out that Moses, one of God's prophets, had come before the world with the miracles of the Staff and the White Hand — clear proof of his being a genuine prophet. Jesus, they added, had made the blind see and had healed lepers, again proving by these miracles that he was a prophet of God. Other prophets, too, had been given the power to perform miracles, and they had not hesitated to display this power as a proof of their prophethood. "Tell us," they said, "what miracle have you brought as proof of your prophethood?"

The Prophet listened in silence to what they had to say, then he read out these concluding verses of the third chapter of the Quran:

In the creation of the heavens and the earth, and in the alternation of night and day, there are signs for men of sense; those that remember God when standing, sitting and lying down, and reflect on the creation of the heavens and the earth (saying): 'Lord, You have not created these in vain. Glory be to You! Save us from the torment of the Fire. Lord, those whom You will cast into hell shall be put to eternal shame: none will help the evil-doers. Lord we have heard a preacher call men to the true faith, saying: 'Believe in your Lord,' and we believed. Lord, forgive us our sins and remove from us our evil deeds and make us die with the righteous (3:193).

By reciting these verses, the Prophet meant to show that the proof of his prophethood lay in the universe spread all around us. The whole system of the heavens and the earth testified, albeit silently, to the truth of his prophethood and divine revelation. What further miracle was then required?

The prophethood of the Prophet of Islam was for all time to come. That being so, a miracle of a temporary nature would not suffice to guarantee the genuineness of his mission. His miracle, like his prophethood had to be of a permanent nature, so that even after he had left this world, its benefits would continue to accrue to future generations. That is why the Prophet presented God's world as an enduring miracle in support of his prophethood. The Quran has specified those aspects of the universal system which prove the need for the divine guidance of man on this earth.

The universe is characterized by a question mark after its whole existence; prophethood provides the answer to that question. We have before us a grand and impeccable universe. Not only does it visibly exist, but it is also in perpetual motion; it functions with clockwork regularity and is free of all imperfections. Extremely meaningful activities are taking place within it, and all its component parts are coordinated with total precision. In spite of the incredibly vast and multifaceted expanse which it occupies, it shows absolute perfection in its system of functioning.

On seeing such a universe, one has to ask, "Who is its Creator?" "Who is its Master?" and, "How has all this been brought into being from nothingness?"

The universe puts these questions to us, but it does not give us the answers. It gives us a glimpse of the rainbow without showing us the face of its Creator. There is motion in this world, there is life and there is light. Creativity is at work in every nook and cranny, powered by an all-pervading energy which manifests itself in a great diversity of forms. Many are the life forms in this world, and as many are the 'languages' in which they express themselves, but, as far as the all-important questions are concerned, all remain silent. Neither is there any material thing to give mankind answers to those questions— no signboards on the mountainsides, no special cloud formations in the sky. Here is a riddle which simply cries out for someone to provide us with the answers.

Besides this, an even more difficult question arises as to the ultimate destination of the universe. Everything in it is in motion. The Earth spins on a never-ending journey. The solar system is constantly revolving and, as it does so, takes the Earth and other planets irresistably in one particular direction. The galaxy to which our solar system belongs is also in motion, taking our solar system and other stars on an unending journey through space. The whole universe is on its way to some destination. But there is no part of the celestial caravan which gives us an inkling of where it is going— or even if it will ever come to rest.

This is a question of the utmost importance to man, for he too is part of that celestial caravan. He too is careering towards an unknown destination. Unless he is enlightened as to the nature of his journey and his final destination, his life will be lived in a twilight of doom and uncertainty. This state of affairs demands that there should be some way of giving man this precious information. How else is he to understand the reality confronting him?

Another important question which is closely related to this is what man should, and should not do. All human beings find themselves in situations where more than one line of action is possible. Which of these are they to choose, and what standards must they set themselves in order to make the best choice? Human beings are not like water, whose course is determined for it by the ups and downs of the land it is crossing. They are not like the stars who move according to a certain order without having to give any thought to it. Nor are they like the trees whose skywards growth is not of their own choosing. Unlike the objects of the universe, which are never faced with options, man has always to think of what to do, how to do it, what to take and what to leave. Because of the will and power with which he has been invested, he finds himself eternally confronted with moral dilemmas. Man, in fact, is the only being in the universe for which a definite course of action has not been laid down.

Functioning with perfect regularity, the sun daily gives us light, but it does not throw any light on the question of our lives. Winds blow all over the world, bringing the fragrance of the flowers to our nostrils, but they do not bring us any news concerning the basic issues confronting us. Water remains liquid, freezes, turns into vapour all in accordance with a definite law. It provides us with coolness and moisture. It is the most refreshing of all drinks. But it does not aid us at all in our quest for the truth. The Earth unfailingly rotates upon its axis, thereby removing the veil of night and bringing to us the light of day. But it does not lay bare to us the secret of life. Trees burst upwards through the surface of the earth, to go to work like some highly efficient factory, providing us with nourishment and shade, but they give us nothing with which to nourish our minds. The birds cheer us with their melodies, never in doubt themselves as to which course to adopt. But no message do they pass on to us in a language we can understand.

Stars and planets keep faithfully to their path, never deviating by a single second from their heavenly schedule. Yet they do not reveal the goal towards which mankind is meant to strive.

Everything in the universe, from tiny ants to vast constellations, adheres to a single definite course, and, judging from the way all things are faithful to the pattern laid down for them, they are fully aware of the course they are meant to steer. Only man remains in ignorance of his course of action. In this, he stands alone in the universe— an unaware creature adrift in an all-knowing Cosmos. He sees everything proceeding in due course towards its destination, but, as for himself, he has no idea of what he should do, or where he should go.

Another, more important characteristic which distinguishes man from the rule-bound objects of the universe is that he has the power to do as he wills, launching himself on this or that course of action, or refraining from it altogether, as he chooses. The Earth rotates on its axis and travels in its orbit without infringing upon the domain of other planets. With man, things are very different. While all things in the world are geared in a certain direction, man is the only being with the capacity to proceed in more than one direction so that when man leaves his own domain, he often encroaches upon those of his fellow-men. This fact alone shows that a man must chalk out his course of action in a way very different from the remainder of the Universe. The denizens of the animal and vegetable kingdoms have an innate knowledge of their path, just as celestial objects have their appointed course. But man is not born with this knowledge, and must find it elsewhere.

History, sad to say, has demonstrated man's inability to seek out the correct course in life. He may be endowed with a keen intellect and a broad-based understanding, but these have proved woefully inadequate in dealing with the basic issue in life— the question of what course of action to adopt.

No efforts of his own can enable him to arrive at an answer to this question: the experience of thousands of years has shown this to be true.

Not finding any answer to his question in the world around him, man started delving into the matter himself, but whole generations of truth-seekers have failed to arrive at any convincing conclusions. Man may have discovered the principles underlying the motion of the stars and planets, but he has not been successful in finding out anything about his own life's journey— where it began, and where it will all come to an end. He has discovered the laws of the animal, vegetable and mineral worlds, but the law of man himself has remained a mystery to him. He has grasped the fact that when matter is destroyed, it converts into energy, which then turns into matter when destroyed itself. But what happens to a man after death? No answer to this question has so far been furnished by the human intellect. Man has discovered that all objects in the universe are governed in their behaviour by one unchanging law, and that they have continued to function for millions of years without once deviating in the slightest from the dictates of this law. But, as for the law which guides man in his life— he has remained in the dark as to what this may be. Using the most advanced equipment, man has gazed into the outer reaches of space and delved deep into the internal workings of the tiniest of atoms. But he has not been able to gain any insight into the reality of man, or even according to what Plan he has come into the world.

To find out about himself is man's greatest need, yet, in this, he is quite helpless. His very helplessness shows that he is in desperate need of someone to guide him. Herein lies the conclusive proof of the necessity for prophethood. Without prophetic guidance, man is unable to make his life meaningful. The sheer necessity of prophethood for man is further confirmed by the teachings of the prophets which provided complete and, therefore, satisfactory answers to all the questions confronting man: they are, in themselves, a proof that the prophets were sent into the world by God, and that they derived their knowledge from Him. One of the most important features of their mission is to explain the divine laws by which man must allow his existence to be governed, for, unlike the non-human creature of this world, man has no innate knowledge of the laws to which he must conform.

The crucial point made by the Prophet of Islam is that this universe has One God who, with His extraordinary strength and wisdom, controls and sustains it. In order to understand how perfectly satisfactory this explanation is, let us imagine a complex piece of machinery which runs with perfect precision, but which bears no inscription which would give us a clue as to its origins. Onlookers, amazed at its masterly construction, would dearly like to know the name of the manufacturer. Their curiosity is at last set at rest when an informed person names the most advanced factory in the entire field of engineering as its place of manufacture. This quite adequately explains how all its parts happen to work with such smooth coordination.

Likewise, our wonder at the impeccable functioning of our colossal universe and our curiosity about how it came into existence are satisfied by the Prophet's explanation that there is one all-powerful God, who has created this world and who guides it on its journey by means of His divine power. We find this answer acceptable because it is in no way far-fetched. Belief in God, in fact, is in no essential way different from belief in ourselves. At the purely human level, we apprehend ourselves as beings who see, hear, think, move around, use their hands and their brains, make plans, make things happen in the world, and so on. Just this experience of ourselves tells us that human beings are invested with certain powers, albeit in limited form. What then is so extraordinary about these same powers being embodied, to absolute perfection, in an all-powerful

God? The relative scales on which these powers are enjoyed may be widely different but, in essence, the powers remain the same. The "I am" that everyone understands in everyday life is the very statement which proves that "God is."

The other certainty which the Prophet brings to us is that this universe has a definite end which will become manifest to us after death. He makes it clear also that the power which man appears to wield in this world has been granted to him only for a certain limited period of time so that he may be put to the divine test. When this period is over, the present Order will be replaced with a new and perfect one, and, whereas God is now hidden from our view, He will at that time become manifest in all His might and majesty. If He remains concealed from us at the present time, it is so that we may the more effectively be put to the test. Everyone is given the opportunity to make the most of his or her time in this world, but it is only those who proved faithful to God, when God was as yet hidden from the world, who will receive God's blessings to the fullest extent in the world that is to come. Those who remained at a distance from God in this world will find themselves far removed from His blessings in the eternal world of the afterlife.

The word of the Prophet is the ultimate truth, for, is it conceivable that God should create a sensate being such as man without His ever appearing before him to allow him to see and know his Lord?

It is likewise inconceivable that a world which appears so meaningful to us should have no just conclusion, and that there should not come a day when wrongdoing and injustice are exposed for what they are. Here, once again, the message that the Prophet brings us about the Day of Judgement strikes a welcome chord in the human heart. In a world where things come into being from nothingness, as it were, where day follows night, where mighty trees spring

40

from tiny seeds, where today is always followed by tomorrow, we should have no difficulty in accepting the idea of a hereafter. It is like the breaking of a new day, but on a wider horizon than the daybreak we witness with our own eyes in this world. Once we have had it put to us in this way, we find it quite easy to accept the coming of an even greater tomorrow than that which comes to us daily with the rising of the sun. The word of the Prophet converts what we feel should happen into a conscious conviction. It puts the stamp of certainty on an event which is only hinted at by the happenings of this world.

Human beings, by their very nature, desire a definite focus for their attention, some point upon which they can concentrate their thoughts and emotions. This is a continual need which is felt by all. Some meet this need by giving all their attention to their wives and families, to their tribe, clan or country. Some make wealth or power their central purpose in life. Few of these things, however, are deserving of the serious consideration given to them by the majority of the people, and can cause a distinct perversion of what human urges ought to be. None of these things has the capacity to give a man moral support in times of need, and none will improve the prospects of his life having a successful outcome.

The attainment of goals connected with the above-mentioned personal interests is almost invariably, at the expense of another, and this leads to continuous strife in society. What people need is the kind of focus for their attention which will contribute to their own spiritual uplift without causing any harm to others. The prime focus offered to mankind by the Prophet is the worship of Almighty God. This means putting one's trust in Him and fearing Him and loving Him above all else. This is a course of action which has been made easy for us to understand by the Prophet's showing us how God, unlike finite matter, is infinite not only in His power but in His accessibility. He has

41

made it plain that there can be no worthier focus of our attention; his advocacy of this cause supports his claim that he has been sent to the world by God.

One of the major afflictions of human society is that no matter how fautlessly its laws are formulated, there are always people who will find loopholes in them. The wielder of power defies the law, the rich man buys 'justice' and the clever manipulator conceals his wrong - doing or displays it in a favourable light. The cheats and twisters of truth are legion. When human beings deal with other human beings without any reference whatsoever to God, all kinds of malpractices are to be expected. But the moment God becomes the true focus of attention, all such ignoble activity ceases outright. When one is dealing with God, from whom nothing can be hidden, one steps warily, and with due regard for one's fellow-men. We should never lose sight of the fact that the law can never be upheld unless there is the kind of respect for it which is rooted in the fear of God.

The essential factor in the making of a sound world order is the spirit of self-sacrifice. What does such sacrifice entail? It means giving precedence to the opinions of others, seeing the credit due to oneself given to others, putting others' interests before those of one's own household, and even handing over one's own hard-earned wealth to others, or expending energy on apparently thankless tasks. Without this spirit of sacrifice, society degenerates into a den of deceit and plunder. It is when people believe that there is no other life but the life of this world that they have no incentive to be self-sacrificing. Without God as the focus of attention, society is inevitably torn with strife, making it impossible for a harmonious environment ever to develop on earth.

The Prophet, however, shows mankind a different and better destiny, one which is based on the worship of God and the self-sacrifice which that entails. Moreover, he makes people realize that their sacrifices are not a senseless waste, for they will be fully rewarded in the afterlife. When people begin to realize what value their right action will have in the eyes of God, they will root out all injustice from society and lay down a solid foundation for truth and justice. Everyone will then be ready to sacrifice his own interests, without which no stable and upright society can come into existence. The religion brought by the Prophet of Islam is no different from that brought by his forerunners. Its only distinguishing feature is that, whereas the previous religions could not survive intact after the passing of their prophets, that of Islam has been preserved in its pristine form right down to the present day. It was because the followers of previous religions were not powerful enough to preserve their religion in its original form that God sent the Prophet of Islam as the final prophet to the world, and helped him to gain ascendancy over all other nations and religious denominations. The success of the Prophet was indeed extraordinary, giving tangible proof that he was truly a prophet of God, for such success has not been the lot of any other individual throughout the entire history of the world. Such an incomparable victory could never have been within the grasp of an ordinary human being, and it was only with divine assistance that the Prophet could triumph in the way he did.

The victory of the Prophet of Islam over his enemies and the success enjoyed by his mission, both in and outside Arabia, are unique events in world history. This is a fact accepted by reputed historians who freely admit that the Prophet's success has never been equalled either before or after him. Even those who do not believe in him feel compelled to put the Prophet's name at the top of any list they compile of great figures in world history.

The Prophet's unique and exceptional success is usually categorized as a human achievement, pure and simple, thus entitling him to lavish praise as a great personality. But there is obviously more to his success than this, for if it was nothing more than a 'human achievement' in the normal sense of the expression, why is it that no other human being has been able to equal it? There should have been nothing to prevent other figures in history from winning similar or even greater victories. The truth of the matter is that the exceptional nature of the Prophet's success is a sign of the most tremendous significance: it is a sign of his having had God's assistance in whatever he did. It was because he was God's prophet, God's representative on this earth, that the Almighty gave him His divine succour. The exceptional success he achieved proved him over and over again not only to be an outstanding human being but to be the true Prophet of God.

What is even more important is that the Prophet's success laid the ground work for the permanent preservation of the religion he brought. The triumph of his progress made it possible for his followers to found an empire extending over a vast area, and this in itself ensured the perpetuity of the Prophet's religion. It is truly remarkable that fourteen hundred years have elapsed since the coming of the Prophet without his religion having been altered in the slightest way. It has been preserved in all its purity, exactly in the form in which the Prophet presented it to the world. In the past, the need for a new Prophet had always arisen because God's religion, suffering from the vagaries of time had been frequently distorted from its original form. In ancient times, the nations who had been entrusted with the guardianship of the Divine Scriptures repeatedly betrayed that trust, allowing the Book of God to be laid waste. New Prophets, therefore, had to come to the world time and time again in order to revivify the true spirit of religion and to re-introduce its teachings in their true form to mankind. But after the Prophet of Islam, the world will see no further prophets, for the Book which the Prophet gave to the world— the Quran— is still fully preserved in its original form.

It is not only the Prophet's Scripture which is with us today, but his very own spirit. It is as though he himself were still amongst us as a living Prophet, for his utterances, the events of his life, the struggle of his prophetic mission, have all been fully recorded and have remained, intact. Thanks to the advent of the modern printing press, authentic renderings of his thoughts and actions can be read and appreciated all over the world. It is an absolute certainty that he will remain God's Messenger to mankind for all time to come.

4

The Hereafter

There are many instances in Hadith literature of the unerring justice of divine retribution for, in the life after death, man will be rewarded or punished strictly in accordance with the virtues or vices of his deeds in this world.

The Quran gives us this notable example: "Proclaim a woeful punishment to those that hoard up gold and silver and do not spend it in God's cause.   The day will surely   come when their treasures shall be heated in the fire of Hell, and their foreheads, sides and backs branded with them. Their tormentors will say to them;"These are the riches which you hoarded, taste then the punishment which is your due" (9:34-35).

When the Prophet went on his Night Journey to the Heavens, amongst the things that he was shown was a world of allegory in which man's worldly actions appeared in an other-worldly form. He was not only shown the results of good deeds in the everlasting life after death, but was also given an insight into the forms which evil deeds would assume in that eternal world.

When he saw people having their heads smashed with mighty rocks, he asked the Archangel who they were, and was told that they were those whose heaviness of head prevented them from rising for prayer. Then there were people grazing in the manner of cattle, with patches all over their clothes. When he asked who they were, the Archangel told him that they were the ones who did not spend their wealth to advance God's cause. Then he saw someone trying to lift a bundle of wood he had gathered, but each time he was on the point of doing so, a few more sticks would be added to the bundle. This time the Prophet was told that this was a man who, instead of trying to diminish an already overwhelming load of responsibilities, took more and more of a burden upon himself.

Others were having their tongues and lips cut with scissors. The Angel accompanying the Prophet explained to him that these were people whose tongues wagged uncontrollably and irresponsibly, causing corruption in the land. In one place the Prophet saw a huge ox emerging from a hole in a rock. When it tried to re-enter it, it was unable to do so, even after a mighty struggle. When the Prophet asked what this meant, the Angel told him that this represented a person who, having uttered contentious words and seen their evil consequences, wanted to take back his words but was unable to do so. At another point, people were cutting off pieces of their own flesh and eating them. The Prophet was told that these were the ones who accused and derided their fellow men.

Next were individuals whose nails were made of copper. With these they were scratching their own faces and chests. These turned out to be people who sought to expose the faults of others, attacking their honour and dignity. There were some too, with lips like those of camels, consuming fire. The angel told the Prophet that they were the devourers of orphans' property. Then came people with enlarged stomachs full of writhing snakes. Passersby were trampling on them, but they could not escape, for they were rooted to the spot, unable to move. "These," said the Angel, "are the usurers." Further on there were people who had piles of meat placed on both sides of them. On one side was good, fresh meat, and on the other side was rotten, foul-smelling meat. These people, ignoring the good meat, were eating the meat which had gone bad. The Angel explained

47

that these were the men and women who had forsaken their own legitimate spouses and taken to unlawful partners for the satisfaction of their desires."

The state of affairs in Paradise is the same. The Quran explains that the reward given in Heaven will be of the same hue as one's actions in this world. "Proclaim good tidings to those who have faith and do good works. They shall dwell in gardens watered by running streams. Whenever they are given fruit to eat, they will say: 'This is what we used to eat before,' for they shall be given the like" (2:25). This means that the rewards of the Hereafter will be in exact accordance with one's actions in this world. The form of the reward will be exactly suited to our deeds.

At one place during the same Night Journey, the Prophet saw some harvesters at work. The more they cut, the more their harvest increased. When he asked who they were, he was told by the Archangel that they were people who struggled on earth in the path of God.

Man is being tested in this world to see what response he offers in certain given situations. It is man and man alone who is being tested in this way. An inanimate object, such as a stone or a piece of wood, would not find itself required to give responses to varying sets of circumstances. Man, on the other hand, is an aware, sensate being, who is stirred by the situations he faces in life, and who reacts to them mentally and physically, in word and in deed. God has given man freedom of thought and action in this world, and herein lies man's real test, for God has given man this freedom to see how he uses it—whether, for example, he returns abuse for abuse, malice for malice, or whether he suffers these things, yet offering only prayers and goodwill in return.

Man's response to the situations he faces in life can take one of two forms: the infernal or the heavenly. An infernal response is one which is categorically opposed to the will of God, while a heavenly response is one which humbly conforms to His will. Those who make the former response are Satanic in character and fit only for Hell. The latter evince divine characteristics and will be admitted to the Garden of Bliss.

How do we define 'Satanic' characteristics? They are those personality traits which cause an individual to embark on a retaliatory course, quite unmindful of the consequences, whenever he is confronted with circumstances which are not to his liking. Whether it be pain, sorrow or mere embarrassment which is inflicted upon him, he feels he must hit back, returning hate for hate, anger for anger. Divine characteristics, on the other hand, being deeprooted in the fear of God, cause a man to rise above fleeting emotions and prevent him from being swayed by passionate love or hate in his dealings. To acquire these divine characteristics, we need only put into practice the commandments the Prophet was given by his Maker: "To join up with those who sever ties with me; to give to those who deprive me; to forgive those who wrong me."

In this world there is no escaping adverse sets of circumstances in which unpleasantness occurs over and over again, thus arousing strong antipathies. But believers are exhorted, by divine commandments, to rise above the treatment meted out to them and to confront negative treatment with positive behaviour. This means suppressing angry and vengeful feelings, and permitting absolutely no outburst of bitterness and loathing. All of these emotions have to be thoroughly stifled, and, in spite of having experienced them, the true believer must deal with others in the purest spirit of goodwill.

The Garden of Paradise is an exquisite and unblemished haven, which God has specifically created for the truly righteous among His servants. A glimpse of this world is to be had from the words of the Prophet:

"The Companions of Paradise will eat and drink there, but they will neither salivate, urinate or defecate."

49

"What will happen to what they eat?" asked the companions, to which the Prophet replied: "There will be belching and perspiration, which will be as fragrant as musk. Praise and glorification of God will come as naturally to them as breathing comes to you in this world."

Just as the human body excretes filth, so does the human mentality emits hate, antipathy, jealousy, vengeance, arrogance and injustice. Considering that the Prophet's words show Paradise as a world in which all filth and foul matter will be emitted in a fragrant form, how could it ever be possible for people who emit foul sentiments to enter that flawless domain? Those who discharge 'filth' in a form that is unacceptable are certainly not fit to inhabit the pure world of Paradise.

Those of God's servants who will be welcomed in Paradise are those who exude purity. They are the ones who show love in return for hatred, who forgive when they might well seek vengeance. Paradise is a place for people who display good- will when tempted to be jealous and malicious, a sense of justice when in a position to be cruel, and humility when it would be easy to be arrogant. This is what is meant by transforming inner filth into purity and fragrance. It is only people who are able to do so who will find their abode in the Gardens of Paradise.

The world has been so made that from time to time unpleasant situations are bound to arise. This is inescapable, since the world has been thus designed as a place of trial for mankind. One who responds positively in untoward situations will prove himself worthy of Paradise, while one who allows himself to fall a prey to negative sentiments will forfeit his right even to enter its gates.

Those who are truly fit to breathe the air of Paradise are the ones who, when beset by some calamity, do not succumb to despair, but who bear their sufferings with patience and fortitude. They are the ones who pray for those who wrong them, who adhere to justice and give others whatever is their due. They do not resent being critcised, but rather listen to their critics dispassionately. No matter how great their grievances, they do not waver from the path of justice. Justice, in fact is the hallmark of their behaviour towards others; all can expect exemplary treatment at their hands. Although feelings of resentment and antagonism may creep into their hearts, because they themselves have suffered from disagreeable treatment, they do not allow such feelings to permeate their entire consciousness, and certainly do not permit them to affect their outward demeanour. Indeed, they make extra efforts to convert all feelings of antipathy into good-will and fair-mindedness before having any further dealings with those who have wronged them. They behave like the flowers which counter pollution with fragrance. The only people who can live such utterly blameless lives are those who remember God with every breath they take and whose hearts beat to the tune of their Maker. The lives of such saintly people are, indeed, based on the twin pillars of fear and love of the Lord.

When the flames of contumacy are fanned, it is the believer's duty to bow in humility. When there is an upsurge of hatred, a believer should extend his kindness and love. Wherever ill-will is in evidence, a believer is required to be the embodiment of good-will and benevolence. When imprecations are being hurled, it is a believer's duty to utter words of prayer. There are times when one is tempted to deny the rights of others: at such times, the believer must not forget the demands of justice, and must give others what is theirs by right. There are times too, when to acknowledge the truth is to suffer a loss of face; even so a believer should banish all thoughts of personal position and prestige, and acknowledge the truth, no matter how painfully humiliating. Sometimes there is an urge to have one's revenge, at such moments, a believer is duty-bound to suppress this urge and to act in a manner which is in total consonance with the principles of justice and the sentiment of good-will.

If one is riding in a lorry, one cannot avoid experiencing a series of jolts as the lorry bounces along. A luxury car, on the the other hand, no matter how fast it is travelling, gives its passengers a smooth, comfortable journey, thanks to its shock-absorbers. It is because the lorry has no shock absorbers of this type that it passes on all the jolts to its passengers. A man who does not fear God is like that lorry. Unable to bear his own psychological jolts, he passes them on to others. One who fears God, however, absorbs the jolts himself, thus preventing others from being disturbed by their impact. Living on this earth amongst other human beings, one is bound to have unpleasant experiences from time to time. The man who patiently acts as a buffer to these shocks, thus preventing others from suffering their impact, is a person of very great merit. But the person who can absorb unpleasant experiences and then pass them on to others in the form of pleasant experiences is of even greater merit. It is people with such patience, fortitude and consideration for others who are truly fit to take up residence in Paradise— a place of the greatest purity and refinement, where even filth impinges on the senses in the form of fragrance. The best candidate for entry to such a world is one who has shown his capacity to accomplish this same process of conversion in the world of mankind. Here, the manifestation of filth in the form of fragrance takes place on an abstract level, within the mind. In Paradise, at God's behest, it will assume a physical form. In other words, human action on a moral plane in this world will take concrete shape in the next world.

Every situation which confronts a man in this world invites one of two kinds of responses. It is on the basis of this response that one will be pronounced fit for Heaven or for Hell.

A true word is spoken. One acknowledges it, another denies it. An issue arises, eliciting justice and mercy on the one hand, and cruelty and oppression on the other. Adverse circumstances come into being, arousing feelings of humility in one and contumacy in another. Attitudes of good-will and regard for others are faced off by the urge to hate and avenge. These opposing reactions are what determines our fate in the Hereafter, the positive taking us to Heaven and the negative to Hell. We should never lose sight of the fact that it is by them that we stand, or fall.

5

The Five Pillars of Islam

Islam, according to the Prophet, was built upon five tenets: "The sworn testimony that none is worthy of being served besides God and that Mohammad is His servant and Apostle; ritual prayer; the giving of alms; pilgrimage to the House of God, and the fast of Ramadhan."

A building, when looked at in the mass, appears to be the sum of its many intricate parts. But what is it which bears aloft the entire soaring edifice? One comes inevitably to the pillars, the underpinnings of the whole structure. Thus, the above-cited articles of faith, are, figuratively speaking, the "pillars" of Islam, without which the entire Islamic edifice would come crashing to the ground.

Human individuals are like pieces of land on which such an edifice can be raised. But, if that edifice is to be pleasing to God, it must be set firmly on those five pillars of Islamic tradition. Without this, the structure of Islam cannot be built up and supported at the level either of the individual or of society.

According to Islam, all individuals should lead lives of worship of and devotion to God. The different observances which are the warp and weft of such an existence—faith, prayer, fasting, charity, pilgrimage – are not mere rituals, but are integral virtues of the Islamic awareness. Faith, to take the most important, is, in essence, belief in the truth of divine realities. Prayer is an exercise in physical and mental prostration before God, such as will banish all notions of personal greatness. Fasting - perhaps the most difficult - teaches one to be steadfast in one's trust of God. Charity entails the recognition of others' claims upon one, so that one shall not forfeit one's own share in God's bounty. Lastly, the pilgrimage serves to unite God's servants around their Maker. Once an individual attains the high degree of piety engendered by the observance of these Islamic requirements, he can be judged to have acquired such characteristics - selflessness, patience, readiness to acknowledge the rights of others - as will gain him God's blessings for all time to come.

Faith

When one finally acknowledges God as one's Lord and Master, one is entering, as it were, into a 'contract' with God, a covenant which excludes all other beings and makes Him all in all. Then it is around Him alone that all one's thoughts and emotions will revolve; it is in Him alone that one will place complete trust. With the passage of time it will be to no one but the Almighty that all one's hopes, fears and supplications will be addressed.

There is no one - great or small - who does not have a focus of attention and activity in his life. For some, the household and family hold the central position, while for others it is business and money-making. For yet others, the preoccupations of political leadership are all that matter. Many base their entire lives on dreams of power and prestige. But, whatever the sources of human satisfaction, if a man does not live in his Lord, his life will be one of the most abysmal ignorance and vacuity. He will have built himself a house of straw, to be carried away by the merest puff of wind. It is only when he strenuously pulls himself out of his mundane existence, and begins to live in his Creator that he will discover what in esence his true life ought to be. It is only then that he will understand his

Maker's intentions, and realize that he is now in possession of that divine support without which, not only he, but the entire universe would collapse. Once he has achieved that state, he will think of God day and night, as he sleeps and as he awakens, and will not take the slightest initiative without first putting his trust in God. It will be for God and God alone that he will speak or remain silent.

Faith can be likened to the electric current which lights up the factory and sets all machines in motion. When faith comes to a man, it is like the arrival of the electric current from the power house – his soul is ablaze with light, his heart throbs faster with devotion, and a new fire – zeal – burns within him; his entire being is stirred with a longing for his Lord. This human being, born of his mother's womb, is born once again from the womb of faith.

When two people love one another, they remain with each other mentally and emotionally, even if they are thousands of miles apart. Physical separation does nothing to impair the quality of their attachment for each other, and, in each and every thing, they see a likeness of the beloved's face. A similar emotional bond links the true believer with God, so that when confronted with the vastness of space, he will behold, not emptiness, but the greatness of the Lord. In the fury of the tempest he will see the glory of his Maker. When birds sing, he will hear divine melodies, and when the sun peeps over the horizon, he will experience its warmth and light like a caress from the hand of his Lord. The sight of the beautiful foliage of the trees, will make him feel that God has spread out the story of His creation before him in every leaf, twig and bud. The merest breath of wind in his face will make him feel that he has come closer to God. In fact, at every instant, the believer in God is bathing in a divine ocean of unfathomable depths. Each experience serves to strengthen his bond with the Lord. God and he become as one.

To believe in God is to have faith in One who is

Creator, Master and Sustainer of the Universe. It is He who has fashioned all things; there is nothing which can function except by virtue of His power; without Him, nothing can even begin to exist. Faith awakens human consciousness to this great truth and man, in his new-found awareness, sees himself as the slave of the Almighty. All things appear to him as manifestations of the Lord and, whatever it falls to his lot to receive, he cherishes as a divine gift. He is unceasing in his praise and rememberance of the Lord.

The individual who is thus imbued with faith is not negligent in the way he lives on earth, remaining alert to every opportunity of coming closer to his Lord, for he is ever aware of the many blessings showered on him by his Creator. For instance, when his fatigue of the previous day has been banished by a good night's rest, he expresses his profound gratitude for this miracle called sleep. Without sleep one would go mad and soon die. When he sees the darkness of the night dispelled by the rising sun, he exclaims quite involuntarily: "Blessed be the One who has created light! Without light the entire world would be plunged into a sea of pitch darkness!" And just the satisfaction of his hunger and the quenching of his thirst floods his whole being with a sense of gratitude. Amazed at the miracles of food and water, he falls to wondering what state mankind would be reduced to, were it not for such blessings sent down by the Almighty.

When the believer is hurt, it is to God that he calls out for comfort and consolation; when he is in distress, it is to God that he turns for help. Whenever he has stood to gain, he is ever-mindful of the fact that this is part of the Lord's bounty, and is moved to offer Him his heartfelt gratitude. Should he incur a loss, he bows to the reality that all things happen at the will of God. He does not become arrogant when showered with blessings, neither is he driven to despair by the adversity of conditions. The strength of his attachment to his Lord is so great that not even the most wonderful of attachments to another human being can impair it. Neither can any greater or lesser degree of self-interest divert him from his duty to the Almighty.

From time to time, important scientific discoveries are made by brilliant minds aided by sophisticated apparatus—the gravitational force of the earth and cosmic rays being two of the better known. But although their impact is very great in the realms of science, they do not saddle either the discoverers, or the recipients of their new-found knowledge, with any significant moral responsibilities. Nor do they bring any keener awareness of the ultimate reality. No matter how scientifically important they may seem as forms of enlightenment, they cannot compare with the discovery of God.

Discovering God means arriving at the source of all strength and wisdom. It is the meeting of the soul with the one who is all-hearing, all-seeing and all-knowing. With the discovery of our Maker comes the consciousness that He has not created this universe in vain. How could such a great universe for ever remain a mystery? Is it within the realms of possibility that its meaning should never become manifest? In a universe controlled by a God who is both omniscient and omnipotent, this is simply inconceivable. To one who has made the discovery of faith, the certainty inevitably comes that God, who had hitherto directed the world from behind the scenes, will stand forth in all His glory, to be emblazoned on every cloud, crag and pinnacle, on every blade, leaf and twig, on every heart, body and soul. On that day of days, doubts and differences will be banished forever, and the truth will belong to all. This conviction brings the believer to the further conclusion that when the Creator and Master of the Universe ultimately takes on a visible form before all His creatures, this manifestation will have direct, personal repercussions on every human soul. It will not be an event which can be viewed dispassionately as if it were just another natural phenomenon like the rising

58

of the sun or the waxing and waning of the moon, bearing no direct relation to the moral aspect of our lives: it will be an awesome event— the manifestation of a Being, a Power, who is not only possessed of a limitless knowledge of all things, but who is both Reckoner and Retributor. When the Lord of the Universe makes himself manifest, all of His creation will arise from the dead to await His judgement. Those who have rebelled against Him, and those who have thought fit to worship only themselves, will on that day be like men of straw; they will be brought low, lower than the most grovelling of insects. On the contrary, those who have believed in God, devoting their entire lives to Him, will find themselves immediately raised to a superior position. During the millenia on earth when God chose to remain concealed those who were not faithful to Him were free to revel in their apostasy. But when God reveals Himself to them, they will realize how ill-used their freedom was and how abysmal their failure in the eyes of their Maker. It will only be those who remained faithful to Him, invisible as He then was, who will find themselves crowned with success in the after-life. God's manifesting Himself will mark the beginning of a new and perfect world, in which those who were faithful to Him will lead a life of everlasting bliss, and in which those who rebelled against him will be relegated to eternal punishment.

Whenever a human being finally grasps this reality, he trembles in fear of God, He cries out to his Maker: "Lord! Save me from disgrace on that day when you appear in all Your Power and Glory! When I stand helpless before You on that day, only You will hold the scales of justice in your hand; only you shall be the possessor of power."

The very act of having faith in God entails acceptance of the Prophet as His Apostle. This is of the greatest importance, for the moment a man discovers God as a live and conscious Being, he needs to understand what God wants of him; he may garner indications from his own inner nature and from the world all around him, but he needs someone to spell out the Lord's message to him in quite unmistakable terms. In particular, he does not wish to be left in any doubt as to the events of the Last Day, and who is better to explain them to him in advance than God's very own Prophet? It is exactly at this crucial, questing stage of his spiritual development that the words of the Prophet resound in his ears: "I am God's servant and His Apostle. The Lord has sent me to bring guidance to mankind. Come to me and hear the message of God."

The genuine seeker after the truth will have little difficulty in recognizing the Prophet's call, for he will already have broken down the walls of prejudice and indifference which confine the ignorant and the complacent within their cell of spiritual darkness. The truth-seeker will recognize the word of God, as His Prophet brings it to him, just as a child recognizes his own mother's voice. Through the words of the Prophet, he comes truly to know God. His soul blossoms at the very sound of them in the way that drought-stricken land puts forth green shoots as the blessed rain falls from the heavens. His whole inner being becomes radiant as if bathed in a divine light. His discovery of God is raised to an infinitely higher plane of illumination by his discovery of God's Prophet.

The Prophet is neither an angel nor any other kind of supernatural being, having been born into this world of a human mother, just like any of his fellow-men. What truly distinguishes him from the rest of mankind is his having been chosen by God as His messenger. In the Prophet, God saw a man in whom the fires of human nature burnt bright, and in whom there was no contradiction of thought, word and deed. In the forty years before he attained prophethood, he had never once betrayed a trust. He was strictly honest in his dealings, true to his word, and deeply compassionate towards the human beings all around him. Most important of all, he had a profound desire for the truth, which went far and beyond all craving for profit.

In Mohammad, son of Abdullah, (peace and God's blessings be upon him) God found a pure soul, untarnished by self-interest, and totally uncompromising on the question of right and wrong. He saw in him a man seflessly devoted to the discharge of his duties, and one who would never stoop to idolatrous beliefs. Most important, God had found in this desert Arab a genuine seeker after the truth. It could only be such as he who would appreciate to the full the divine revelations with which he would be entrusted, and who would be fully alive to the resultant obligation. It was precisely because this most perfect of men had shown himself to be so consistently virtuous over the first forty years of his life that God chose him as His final Prophet for all mankind. During the ensuing thirty-three years of his prophethood, Mohammad proved that God's trust in him had not been misplaced, for he carried out his prophetic duties with the highest imaginable degree of integrity. There could have been no conceivably superior fulfillment of the responsibilities entailed by prophethood.

It is thanks to the Prophet that God's Book, as communicated to him by God's Angels, has been handed down to us in pure and pristine form, thus making it possible for us to find in His Scriptures a clear description of all those qualities and observances which our Lord requires of us. In the Quran, God converses with us in human language, and, if His words are as clear to us today as at the time of their utterance, it is because of the special care taken by the Prophet and his companions to ensure that God's Book would be preserved in its original form, unmarred by interpolation, alteration or omission.

Not only did the Prophet receive God's Revelations, but he also practised them to perfection throughout his entire life. He thus provided a living example of how Quranic teaching should be followed. It was easy for people to see and understand the examples he set, for he lived the life of any normal family man, mixing freely with people in the town and market place. Like any other ordinary individual he had friends and enemies, and knew what it meant to win or lose, fail or succeed. But what made him different from the ordinary run of men was the sublimity of his character. No matter what situation he found himself in, he always set a shining example. From a position of affluence and security he was reduced to suffering poverty, hunger, pain and rejection— all in the attempt to preach the Faith. But no matter how adverse the circumstances in which he found himself, he never failed to evince this perfection of character. Conversely, when he rose from the level of an ordinary man to become a judge and a ruler, having ultimately set up the pillars of Islam, this excellence of disposition never left him for an instant. Indeed, his entire life was marked by such divine characteristics that it has become a model for mankind for all eternity.

When we go to meet our Lord, we earnestly pray that we shall find favour in His eyes, hoping to live in the Hereafter in the Gardens of everlasting delight. But if we are to merit this fate, we must ascertain from the Quran what God commands, and must observe from the life of the Prophet how God's commands are to be carried out. We must then mould our lives on the divine injunctions recorded in the Quran and on the supreme example of the Prophet's life. This is the true path for great and small alike. Any other course will lead to perdition.

Prayer

Prayer, the second pillar of Islam, entails the worship of God five times a day in the prescribed manner. This mode of worship, laid down for mankind by God through His Prophet, is so all-embracing that one cannot imagine any superior way of worshipping the Almighty.

When the time for prayer comes, the greatness of God is proclaimed in the call to prayer, and the faithful are instructed to assemble for prayer as a matter of their own spiritual uplift. They then perform their ablutions— in so doing reviving their sense of cleanliness— and, fixing their minds on God, they make their way to the mosque, where they all offer prayers together. The prayers are led by an Imam, under whose guidance Muslims are shown how they should lead their lives. In the same way as the congregation make the Imam their leader in prayers, so should all Muslims unite around the Prophet, making him the focal point of their social existence.

The prayer has various stages: bowing low, prostrating oneself, and standing and kneeling before God. In assuming these various postures, the congregation demonstrate their submission to the Lord. When they stand, hands joined in prayer, when they bow low, when they sit reverently before the Lord, when they touch the ground with their foreheads, with each posture they adopt, they renew their covenant of submission to God.

During the prayers, an excerpt from the Quran is read out. One amazing attribute of the Quran is that, no matter which part is chosen and how much of it is recited, its message is clearly conveyed. This is because each page of the Quran is like a summary of the whole. In this way, any short excerpt from the Quran recited in prayer suffices to show what pleases and what displeases the Almighty.

Besides this, the prayers include praise and rememberance of God, supplications to Him and the expression of goodwill towards the Prophet and all believers. The prayers then end with a message of peace to all mankind. Thus constituted, they are both an act of worship and a reminder of God's commandments. They give solace to believers, while creating social consciousness and unity in their ranks. Prayer is not only a symbol of the Islamic life, but also inculcates self-discipline among Muslims. Although the most important aspect of prayer is its being the main point of spiritual contact with God, it also has valuable lessons for us on how to conduct ourselves in our daily lives.

Prayer, as well as being a ritual mode of worship, is an expression of the inner realities of humility before, and devotion to God. The ultimate acknowledgement of another's greatness being the repetition of the words, "He is the Greatest," the words, *Allahu Akbar,* are uttered time and time again in prayer. Verbal acknowledgement is thus made of the absolute quality of God's greatness in comparison to that of ordinary mortals.

Physically, the ultimate recognition of another's greatness is the act of self-prostration; no physical act is more obviously a testament to the greatness of another than this. Performed repeatedly during prayers, it is a practical reminder and a clear demonstration of one's belief in the incomparable grandeur of God. The giving of one's entire attention to God is underlined by turning one's gaze towards the House of God. The direction in which one must face in order to pray is, therefore, of great religious significance, for it not only focuses one's attention on the deity, but also demonstrates that one's very life is turned towards God. Every aspect of one's life, from inner thoughts to outer needs, then becomes truly God-oriented.

When a servant of God bows before his Lord, and does so, not just as a matter of form, but in the spirit of true humility, the effect of his action does not remain confined to the domain, but extends to his everyday existence, pervading it completely. His thinking and actions bear the permanent stamp of his devotions, for it is impossible for a man to fear God and to bow before Him without being influenced thereby in his dealings with others. A true worshipper cannot be humble and meek before God and yet be arrogant and supercilious to his fellow men. He will not, of course, prostrate himself before them, nor will he address the words "You are great" to another person, as he would to God. But he will certainly avoid asserting his own superiority, and instead will adopt a humble demeanour on a parallel with his self-prostration before his Maker. The submission which he expresses in prayer to God becomes a reality in terms of his observance of others' rights. The very act of facing in the correct direction influences him to take a principled stand in his everyday dealings. At prayer in the mosque, he is the epitome of servitude to God: outside the mosque, he is the perfect character — humble in demeanour, morally upright, and kind, considerate and forgiving in all his transactions.

Besides the five daily prayers, there are other prayers, designed for particular times and special occasions, which are intended to supplement them, and to reinforce this state of mind induced by them. There are prayers for the fulfillment of some great need, for the help of God in some difficult task or new venture, (when the supplicant will offer two *rak'āts* of prayer) as well as prayers to be said in the context of extraordinary events or special individual needs. *Tahajjud* is the prayer recited in the early hours of the morning. This time has been chosen as the most peaceful and quiet period in all of the 24 hours, during which it is easier for the devotee to give his wholehearted attention to the substance of the prayer. The fact that he has to forego his sleep in order to recite the prayer inculcates the virtue of self-denial. Then there are the congregational prayers on Fridays and Eid festivals, funeral prayers and many others, such as the prayer to be said on visiting a place for the first time.

The important thing about prayer is that it induces the correct attitude in the devotee, as though the spirit of his prayers were keeping a watchful eye on everything he says and does. When going about his worldly affairs, it is as if the whole world were a mosque; his actions, therefore, at all times and in all places cannot be other than in consonance

65

with what his worship requires of him.

Fasting

The ritual of fasting, the third pillar of Islam, is observed each year by Muslims throughout the entire month of Ramadhan, the ninth month of the Muslim calender. The period of fasting each day lasts from the first light of dawn until sunset, thus obliging devotees to make radical changes in their entire daily routine. Since no food or drink whatsoever is to be consumed during daylight hours, they experience the sharp pangs of hunger and thirst, and the fatigue and weakness which accompany them. This abstinence, day after day, from the basic essentials of life teaches a lesson in endurance; it is this willing submission of devotees to the hardships of fasting which strengthen their capacity for patience and fortitude.

In spite of the physical handicaps imposed by fasting, they remain alert, discharging their duties and carrying out their responsibilities. When they see food and water before them, feel tempted to eat and drink, but then refrain from doing so, their will-power is strengthened each time they resist temptation. In this way, they prepare themselves to lead a disciplined and responsible life, in which they do what is right and eschew what is wrong. Despite the difficulties strewn in their path, they press on towards the achievement of the true Islamic goal of life.

God has bestowed innumerable blessings upon man in this world— the air, the light of the sun, the rain, the water of rivers, lakes and seas being the most basic to his needs. But because these things come to man with little or no effort on his part, he tends to take them for granted. He does not see them for the great blessings that they are. He does not pause to consider how all of them have been specifically created to meet his own precise needs. Were one of these amazing blessings to be completely withheld, life would become intolerable. It is only when he observes the ritual of fasting that he truly realises their significance and has a proper sense of gratitude for them. It is when, in the evening, after a day of hunger, thirst, exhaustion and discomfort, a man consumes food and drink, that his awareness of God's bounty is most intense. That is when he feels truly grateful to the Creator and Sustainer of life. Were he to give up his whole life to the service of God, he would feel that it was nothing compared to the limitless blessings bestowed on him by his Maker.

The life which a believer is required to live on earth is, from beginning to end, a life of patience. He must confine himself to what is lawful and keep his distance from what has been decreed unlawful by the Almighty. In adhering to the path of truth, he is bound to face difficulties in life. But he must bear with them, and avoid wasting precious time in reacting to the hurdles placed in his way by others. In this way he will be able to persevere in his life's duties in spite of all obstacles. Impervious to the losses incurred by him in this world, he will press on in quest of the gains of the next world. Even when his pride is severely wounded, and the unpleasantness of events causes him great irritation, he refrains from displaying a negative reaction and continues to pursue positive ends. None of this can be achieved without the virtues of patience and endurance.

The path of Islam can be followed only by those who have unlimited reserves of patience, and it is precisely this virtue which is inculcated by the annual lesson of fasting. This lesson, painfully learned during the month of Ramadhan, stays with devotees throughout their entire lives.

The whole life of a believer is, in a sense, a life of fasting: he is required to abstain not just from food and drink, but from anything which is wrong, such as negative thinking, ill-conceived and hastily executed initiatives, in fact, any practice which might prove injurious to others. He is also to refrain from attempting to make lawful that which

67

God has disallowed. Abstinence of this nature comes more easily to those who have undergone the rigours of fasting, than to those who have led a life of unrestricted self-indulgence. Fasting, in short, chastens the soul and strengthens the will to do good.

Zakat

The fourth pillar of Islam, *zakat,* is the giving of alms out of one's own private means at a minimum fixed rate of 2.5% per annum. This money is given in the name of God and is to be spent on worthy religious causes and on meeting the needs of the poor and the helpless.

Zakat is in the nature of an annual reminder to man that everything he possesses belongs to God, and that nothing should, therefore, be withheld from Him.

Man himself plays only a very small part in obtaining whatever he owns in this world. Were he not to have the benefit of God's endless bounty, he would neither be able to grow grain, raise cattle, set up industries nor accomplish any other work of a useful nature. The system of life created for him by God, meeting as it does all of his requirements from those of his inner being to those of his external environment, is one of the greatest perfection. Were God to withdraw even a single one of His blessings, all man's schemes would lie in ruins and all his efforts would be in vain. All productivity would grind to a halt, and life itself would come to a standstill.

The observance of *zakat* is a way of acknowledging this fact of life. Islam desires that private wealth should be considered as belonging to God, and that He should have his rightful share in whatever gains are made. Although a minimum donation has been stipulated, there is no limit to the amount of money which can be given to support God's rightful cause. It is the practice then for Muslims to set aside a certain sum annually, and to donate it to some worthy cause.

In so doing, no one should consider that he is confering a great favour upon those less well-endowed than himself, and should in no way be condescending to the recipients of his charity. When a man gives alms to others, he should do so in the knowledge that they have a rightful share in his wealth, for this is as God has ordained. He is doing no more than give others their due. But when he gives, he can feel reassured that he himself will be given succour by his Maker on the Day of Judgement. In giving to others, he knows for certain that he will not be denied by God at the Last Reckoning.

Zakat gives a clear indication of what one's responsibilities to others should be. Everyone is required to recognize the rights of others, just as everyone is expected to sympathize with those afflicted by adversity. This feeling should be so well developed that one has no hesitancy about sharing one's possessions with others, or coming to their assistance, even when it is clear that nothing can be expected in return. Even where there are no ties of friendship, one should wish others well and guard their honour as if it were one's own.

Zakat brings the realization that all of one's possessions are gifts from God and makes one more keenly aware of the virtues of devotion to God. In the light of such awareness, one cannot remain insensitive to the needs of the society in which one lives. *Zakat* is a perennial reminder that a selfish stance is a wrong stance, and that others must be given their rightful share of our earnings.

One unfortunate aspect of human relationships is that people tend to give to others only when they hope to gain something in return. Money, they feel, should be returned with interest. When such an understanding becomes a factor in our social organization, exploitation becomes rampant; everyone is ready to plunder everyone else. This results in society falling a pray to oppression and disorder.

No one— whether rich or poor — can be at peace in a society stricken with this malaise.

Society should be so ordered that the fortunately placed in life come to the assistance of their less fortunate brothers, in the knowledge that they will ultimately be rewarded by God. Believers have the assurance of God that if they give to others, whatever they give will be returned to them many times over in the next world; their trust in God's promise is complete. In a society ordered in this way, feelings of antagonism and indifference are not allowed to develop: people are not bent on exploiting one another. There is never an atmosphere of mutual resentment and dissatisfaction, for everyone lives in peace with his neighbour. Such a society, in short, is a haven of contentment and well-being.

In its external form then, *zakat* is an annual tax. But in essence, it is the principle on which God and his creatures have a right to a share in one's property.

Hajj

Hajj, the fifth pillar of Islam, is the name given to the pilgrimage to Mecca, the focal point of Islam, where once every year Muslims from all over the world gather to perform a special type of congregational worship. This takes the form of a symbolic enactment of certain Islamic teachings, the observance of which is a requirement on both spiritual and material levels, since it demonstrates the individual's readiness to put Islamic precepts into practice in his everyday life. Individual acts of Islamic worship may be similarly defined, but the scale on which they take place during Hajj and their close combination produces an intensification of their overall effect. Individual pilgrims then have a sense of belonging to a unified whole.

The ideal of all men living on earth as God's servants, and therefore as equals, is expressed in the wearing of *ihram*

70

(a very simple form of clothing) by all pilgrims, irrespective of their nationality. In this way, all artificial, discriminatory barriers are broken down between people from all walks of life.

It is also the earnest wish of Islam that people's lives should revolve around the Almighty, and a symbolic demonstration of this takes place during the pilgrimage in the circumambulation of the House of God. Another ritual involving physical exertion is *sa'i,* which entails a fast-paced walk between the hills of Safa and Marwah. This gives pilgrims a taste of the intensity with which one must press ever onwards along the path of Islam. Devotees who hear the call of God are exhorted to recite repeatedly: "I am at your service Lord, here I am:" this being the perfect expression of Islamic intention.

One of Islam's major goals is that mankind should live in rememberance of that Day when all will be assembled before God. The gathering of the pilgrims on the plain of Arafat is a visible reminder of this crucial moment in the after-life.

Islam sincerely wishes that man should be free of the clutches of the Devil and that they should continually chase the Evil One away.

The casting of pebbles at the stone devils *Rami al-Jamar* gives pilgrims the opportunity to go through the physical motions of a symbolic fight against evil. Islam desires too, that the believer should adhere to the covenant he has made with God, even if this entails the sacrifice of his property or even his life. At Mina, therefore, during the rites of pilgrimage, the pilgrims sacrifice an animal, thus showing themselves ready to make whatever sacrifices are demanded of them. It is also a requirement of Islam that people should patiently endure the inconveniences they have to suffer on account of their fellow-men, and during the Hajj season, pilgrims have innumerable opportunities of displaying their self- restraint. With so many hundreds of

71

thousands of different types of people gathered together in one place, it is inevitable that there should be countless occasions when some are put to inconvenience by others. This is the time that pilgrims are directed to be especially careful not to give vent to anger or irritation, to refrain absolutely from abusing or attacking anyone and to eschew all immodest or dishonest behaviour. Hoping themselves for kind treatment at the hands of God, they do their utmost to be kind in their treatment of other human beings.

Hajj is a rehearsal for a life of struggle in God's cause, a reminder of the momentousness of the Last Day, and a caution that Satan, man's greatest enemy, must be beaten back at all costs. Its greatest message is that if one desires a share in God's blessings, one should be prepared to sacrifice not only one's possessions but one's very life for Him. In this way, it is a lesson in living a God-oriented life.

Through the conditions created at the time of the pilgrimage, people learn how they should live on this earth with their fellow men. They receive a practical exercise in tolerating the difficulties created by others, which makes them realize both the necessity and possibility of living together in a spirit of justice and benevolence. Above all, Hajj is a colossal demonstration of human equality.

It is such a complete act of worship that anyone who performs it in the proper manner will find that it has a salutary effect on all of his or her social interaction, whether in relation to God or to other human beings.

Although we have been commanded to perform Hajj only once in a lifetime, it is such a great and all- encompassing act of worship that, if correctly performed, both in form and in spirit, its impact will be permanent. This once-in-a-lifetime pilgrimage will leave its indelible stamp upon the mind of the pilgrim, thus changing for the better the whole course of his remaining life.

6

The Trial of Man

God created Adam, the first man. He commanded the Angels and the genies (jinns), whom he had created before Adam, to prostrate themselves before him. The Angels hastened to obey this divine commandment, but Satan, the chief of the genies, held himself aloof and did not prostrate himself. When God asked him to explain his disobedience, he replied, "I am better than him: You created me from fire, while him you created from mud." (Quran, 7:12). Since Satan was ready to prostrate himself before God, but not before Adam, he was declared beyond the pale and sentenced to everlasting damnation.

Clearly, in human relationships there are always two main possible courses of action: either to tread the path of acknowledgement of the superiority óf others and to demonstrate our submission to them— as shown by the Angels— or to assert our own superiority over others, with the resulting friction— as shown by Satan. To this day the sons of Adam have to decide whether to side with the Angels, or to become the Devil's comrades, saying of their neighbours: "I am better than he." The drama which was enacted at the time of Adam's creation is still being played out over and over again, in our day-to-day existence, only on a much larger scale.

At some point or the other during our brief sojourn on earth, we are sure to encounter an 'Adam'— one to whom something is due from us, be it only a kindly word. On all such occasions, God makes His will quite plain to us, albeit silently, that, in obedience to Him, we must bow to this Adam. Those who tread the path of the Angels will understand God's wishes and will give their 'Adam' his rightful due, hastening to yield pride of place to him.

It is only people who act in this way who are the true and faithful servants of God. As such, they will find their eternal abode in heaven. Those who follow the example of Satan, and refuse— out of conceit and arrogance— to bow before the 'Adam' who has entered their lives, are rebels in God's eyes. They will be cast into Hell along with Satan, to burn there for all time.

Man being God's servant must prostrate himself first and foremost, before his Master. But in everyday situations, it often happens that in his immediate environment there are individuals who have some claim upon him, or some right to assert over him. These are the 'Adams' before whom he must bow at the behest of the Almighty. This is a test which God sets for man in life. It is an exacting test, because although human beings are quite prepared to bow before God— His superiority being unassailable— they find it difficult to acknowledge the rights of other ordinary individuals, who, they feel are in no way superior to themselves. This is when the 'Satan' in them comes alive and drives them to the perversity of ignoring, or denying the rights of others. They refuse to bow before Adam, despite this being a commandment of that very deity before whom they regularly prostrate themselves. Like Satan before them, they refuse to bow to those whom they consider inferior to themselves. It is the same superiority complex, the same hubris, that held Satan aloof when the Angels were prostrating themselves before Adam—whether they are conscious of it or not—which prevents them from carrying out the will of God.

Suppose a dispute has arisen between two people. The one who is clearly in the right must obviously assume the role of Adam in the eyes of the one who is in the wrong. The very fact that such situations can and do arise is a clear indication that it is God's will that there should be some who should yield to others. It is in the nature of a divine commandment, and compliance with it is for the sake of God and no one else. One who grants that another is in the right, no matter how irksomely pressing his claims may be, is following in the Angels' footsteps, for, when commanded by God, they did not hesitate to bow before Adam. In sharp contrast is the individual who is so full of his own importance that he challenges the rights of others and refuses to give them their due, particularly when the objects of his ill-will are in no position to retaliate. Such a man follows in the footsteps of Satan who, when commanded by the Lord, refused to bow before Adam. There is no point in such a person prostrating himself before God in the hopes of salvation, for God will only look with favour upon his obeisance, if he is equally earnest in bowing before His creation— Adam.

A man who says, "I am ready to throw myself at the feet of my Lord, but I will not bow to Adam," has become the brother of Satan; his self-prostration has no value in the eyes of God, because it is negated by the pride he displays in refusing to bow to Adam. One who allows pride to be the governing factor in his life will find indeed, that none of his actions are acceptable to God.

The story of the first man, which was enacted in the very presence of God, is now being reenacted over and over again in everyday life, but now, the difference is that God has placed a veil between Himself and mankind, so that He shall remain unseen. We do not see God right there before us, but we do have the Holy Book which He bequeathed to mankind— the Quran— and we also have the sayings and traditions of the Prophet Mohammad. We have, moreover, the voice of our own consciences, which tells us every day that we must, in our dealings with others, acknowledge their rights in word and deed. It is as if we heard the exhortation of God: "Fulfill the obligation you have to this, your fellow man." God tells us to bow before 'Adam,' to pay him his due, whether it entails verbal recognition, or material transactions.

We cannot 'hear' God's command as if, physically, it were an auditory experience. But that is all the more reason to open our hearts to it. That is the way to achieve moral success in life. Those who respond to God's command by saying, "I am better than he is," are little better than moral failures. If one responds to God's command as the Angels did, the reward of angels will fall to one's lot, but if one follows Satan, one's fate cannot be other than hellfire and damnation.

If what is actually required of a man is that he should bow before God, how is it possible to tell whether he has truly submitted to God or not? The test of his submission is his willingness to bow before whichever 'Adam' confronts him in life, for the truly devout servant is one who obeys God's commandments by giving other human beings their rightful due. A man who prostrates himself before God, but fails to acknowledge the rights of others, treating them with arrogance and injustice, is only going through a meaningless ritual. When God directs him to bow before another, he is putting him through a test— a test to see whether he is truly the devotee of his Creator. When he fails to bow to that other, he has failed in the test set him by God.

Man is always ready to prostrate himself before God, for who would have the temerity to say of God, "I am better than Him," ? It is only when we have to bow before another human being that our complexes prove a major obstacle. Where God stands alone, and does not admit of anyone being placed on a par with Him, human beings on the other hand, tend to look upon each other as rivals. This being so, one person bowing before another raises the issue of personal prestige.

76

Ever dependent upon His Lord, man bows before Him. God is the giver. Man the receiver. Man never gives anything to God. He has nothing to give. But when man bows to man, that is quite a different state of affairs, for then he does have something to give. It may only be a kindly word that he offers, or, more importantly, it may be the recognition of another's being in the right; sometimes it means handing over a sum of money which is due to another; sometimes it involves withdrawing from some position in recognition of another's superiority; sometimes it is a question of showing respect for someone's honour, by passing over a weakness of his which could have been exploited; sometimes it means holding one's peace, and refraining from pouncing on some mistake that another has made; sometimes it entails siding with someone purely as a matter of principle, eschewing the immediate gain to be had from acting in an unprincipled way. These are all typical situations in which one person must bow to another. In all such cases, the one who accedes to the other is doing something very positive: he is giving something to the other.

There are, of course, a number of mental barriers that have to be overcome before an individual can be completely just and right-minded in his attitude to others. In honouring one's rival, one must often compromise with one's own sense of prestige. This is what really makes it difficult to give precedence to a fellow human being. Yet this is the crucial test set for him by God. Without making this sacrifice, he cannot earn God's favour. One who shirks making this sacrifice can never endear himself to God no matter how many exercises in self-prostration he puts himself through.

A man who achieves a certain superiority owes his position to God. To acknowledge the superiority of another, then, amounts to acknowledging the fairness of God's distribution of His blessings. If one refuses to recognize the superiority of another, that is tantamount to challenging

God's sense of fair play. When one bows before the rights of another, one is not really bowing before another human being, but before God, for it is on account of God's commandment that one bows before that person, rather than because of any excellence inherent in him.

God, the Lord of the Universe, is the Supreme Reality. To discover God is the greatest triumph that a human being can achieve. In this world, it is in the act of self-prostration that a man truly finds his Lord. But such self-prostration is acceptable to God only when a man's entire life is coloured by humility and submission. It is only then that the devotee can be said to be psychologically prepared for being the recipient of God's divine light. His act of self-prostration is the real meeting point with the Lord of the Universe. If, on the contrary, one is arrogant and self-centred in one's day-to-day activities, one's self-prostration is a hollow act, and as such, will not bring one closer to God. Satan will have taken possession of one's heart and one's posture of humility will be bereft of soul. We must never forget that Satan lies ever in wait. "Because you have led me into sin," said Satan,"I will waylay them as they walk on Your straight path, and spring upon them from the front and from the rear and from their right and from their left. Then you shall find the greater part of them ungrateful." "Begone," said God, "a despicable outcast. With those that follow you, I shall fill the pit of Hell."

7

Islamic Character

The truly Islamic character is always marked by humility—the paramount virtue to be cultivated by the believing Muslim.

"The true servants of the Merciful One are those who walk humbly on the earth, and when the ignorant address them, they say: 'Peace!'

(Quran, 25: 63)

The above verse makes it clear that true servants of God are humble in their bearing. This is because, having become aware of their own position in relation to God, they have lost all sense of self-importance. Such people are meek in their dealings not only with God but also with their fellow-men. That humility is the very essence of an Islamic character is illustrated by this saying of the Prophet of Islam:

"Allah has revealed to me that His servants should be humble towards one another. One person is not to commit excesses upon another, nor should one look with scorn upon one's fellow human being."

(Muslim, Sahih)

Hoping for a reward from God.

It is in becoming acquainted with God that one knows what characteristics one should, as a Muslim, cultivate in oneself. Along with the discovery of God, there comes the realization that one is not free to do as one pleases in this world. God's special reason for setting us down in this world for the few years that we are to live out our lives is that He wishes to put us to the test. Then, after death, we will return to Him, and, depending upon how we have behaved while on this earth, we shall either find our eternal abode in Gardens of Delight or else we shall be consigned forever to the raging fires of Hell.

When this reality of life dawns on an individual, his prime concern is then to save himself from God's eternal punishment, and to make himself deserving of His mercy and forgiveness. This concern for his own in the life after death has a direct bearing on his worldly demeanor towards his fellows. He becomes compassionate and forgiving towards others, in the hope that God will in turn shower mercy and forgiveness upon him. He also shows great-heartedness in all his daily transactions, hoping that in this way he will be treated in like manner when he comes before God.

Such is the treatment which a believing Muslim should mete out to others. This has been explained in various ways by the Prophet Mohammed. A selection of his sayings on the subject is given below:

Truly, God shows mercy to those of His servants who are themselves merciful.

Be ready to pardon, so that you may also be pardoned.

Be merciful to those on earth; the One on High will then be merciful to you.

(Al-Jami as-Saghir)

In a long *hadith* related by Abu Hurayrah, the following words of the Prophet appear;

"Whosoever relieves a believer of one of the hardships of this world will himself be relieved of one of the hardships of the Day of Judgment by God; and whoever lightens the burden of one who encounters hardship will have his own burden lightened by God, both in this world and in the next. God helps His servant, so long as that servant is actively helping his brother."

(Muslim, *Sahih*)

All these statements are summed up in a *hadith* related by Jarir, according to which the Prophet said:

"God will not show mercy to one who is not merciful to others."

(Bukhari, Muslim)

Large-heartedness

Say someone hires a taxi and, at the end of his journey, is asked to hand over fifty rupees for his fare. Now, if the passenger has only fifty rupees in his pocket, he is likely to argue that the taxi driver is quoting too high a fare. He does not, after all, want to be left with an empty wallet. However, suppose he has five thousand rupees in his wallet, he will not argue over a mere fifty rupees. He will just pay whatever fare is demanded and go on his way.

The possessor of great wealth will not argue over mere trifles,whereas a man living in straitened circumstances will have to be careful about every rupee he spends. When a man discovers God, it is as if he had suddenly inherited great wealth, and he becomes the biggest-hearted of all human beings. On the other hand, the man who remains distant from his Maker can have no knowledge of this spiritual wealth and, therefore, remains mean-spririted in

81

his dealings with others. The possessor of spiritual wealth develops the capacity to put up with untold losses in this world. Magnanimity becomes the hallmark of his behaviour, as all traces of petty–mindedness vanish from his personality. His is a generous spirit and a sublime nature.

It is this quality which has been attributed to the Prophet Mohammad: "Surely, you have a sublime character" (Quran, 68:4). What does this "sublime character" consist of? It is the capacity always to be guided by high moral principles, and never to act merely on the basis of the treatment one receives from others. A sublime character does not react violently in an adverse situation, nor does it indulge in vengeful retaliation. This is what is known as being 'a man of principle.' It was this type of human being that the Prophet Mohammed urged his followers to become when he warned them not to become *imma'a*. By *imma'a* he meant one who made a point of returning good for good and evil for evil. The Prophet told his followers that they should instead form the habit of being good to those who were good to them, while refraining from wronging those who had wronged them.

The same theme was taken up by the Prophet on another occasion when he said that the finest character out of all the inhabitants of both this world and the next was that of one who forged stronger ties with those who severed their ties with him, who gave to those who denied him and who forgave those who wronged him. The "sublime character" mentioned in the Quran has been interpreted in the same vein. One Quranic commentator says that we should "show forgiveness, enjoin justice and avoid the ignorant" as has been commanded by God in the Quran (7:199). A sublime character then has the capacity to show forgiveness in a situation where revenge might normally be sought; it spreads the message of good-will and justice wherever hate and oppression have taken root, it simply by-passes situation in which there is needless entanglement in disputes.

Two types of character

From the Islamic viewpoint, human character is either noble or ignoble. Those who fall into the latter category do not acknowledge any hard and fast principles which are to be adhered to at all times, preferring to allow themselves to be moulded by particular situations and allowing themselves to be blown in whatever direction the winds of fortune take them. Theirs is an impulsive, changeable, undependable nature.

A man of this type treats with utter contempt anyone whom he considers his inferior, while anyone who appears his superior becomes an object of jealousy. He forges friendships whenever he expects to profit thereby, but adopts an attitude of indifference towards those who do not hold out any promise of advantage. One who treats him well will receive exemplary treatment, but anyone who treats him badly may be sure of even worse treatment in return. If it happens that he succeeds in improving his status, his arrogance knows no bounds. But if high status eludes him, he sinks into despair. He is generous to those he likes, but quite the opposite to those he dislikes. He reserves his praise for those who agree with him, but roundly condemns those who disagree.

These are the different aspects of a degraded character. God and His Prophet have commanded believing Muslims to ennoble their characters by first suppressing all such baseness in themselves.

Nobility of character

The Prophet Mohammad himself was of a very fine character, and he made it his mission to exhort others to cultivate in themselves all that was noble and altruistic. In his *Muwatta,* Imam Malik records the Prophet as saying:

"I have been sent to perfect excellence of character."

In other versions of this statement, the words "righteousness of character" and "graciousness of character" are used. What is meant by this 'graciousness of character' which the Prophet was sent to inculcate? As the Prophet himself made clear in another statement, it consists of three virtues: "Readiness to forgive those who wrong you, to give to those who deny you and to reunite with those who sever their ties with you."

It follows that a sublime character can be formed only when there is never any falling away from high personal standards in the face of wrong treatment from others.

Dependability

When an engineer sets out to build a bridge, he chooses steel as the principal material to be used in its construction (as opposed to wood, bamboo, weaker types of metals, etc) for he knows in advance that it can be depended upon to bear very heavy loads. If he were not at all certain of this, he would not venture to construct a bridge made of steel. Everything in the world has been endowed with certain properties— just as steel has been endowed with strength— and each element can be relied upon to display its own particular properties. The behaviour of each element can, therefore, be predicted when subjected to different sets of conditions. It is because of this reliability of performance in the world of nature that human civilization has been able to advance. Were material objects to lose their properties, the whole edifice of human civilization would fall to pieces.

Such is the importance of the physical properties of the material world. In the human world, too, there are properties which are equally important: they are the elements which together add up to strength of character— a cardinal virtue without which no flourishing society can be built. A society composed of individuals who are weak in character can never be anything but weak itself.

For a society to function in the best possible way, its members should be so dependable that their behaviour under specific conditions should be easily predictable. In other words, in one's dealings with them, one should be able to trust them to do as they say they will do. One should reasonably expect that they will accept the truth and that, even if they have a sense of personal grievance, they will not, therefore, treat others unjustly. Individuals of this nature are true 'men of steel,' for they fulfill the expectations placed in them, just as steel will forever go on bearing the heaviest of loads. A society made up of such people cannot but flourish and progress.

A society in which this is not the case is inevitably doomed to ruin. When people do not keep their promises and refuse to accept the truth when confronted with it, when they take prompt action against others out of a sense of personal grievance, regardless of whether it is humane to do so or not, their society becomes like a world in which steel has ceased to be steel, in which the very rocks have begun to break up into splinters like so much old, rotten wood.

Having others at one's mercy

The severest test of a man's integrity is the realization that he has an enemy at his mercy. Generally, from such a position of advantage, his first impulse will be to destroy the enemy, especially if he considers that the circumstances exonerate him from all moral responsibility.

Even at such moments, however, one who truly fears God will not forget that his Lord is watching over him. His enemy may be in a position of weakness, but this weakness lies under the protection of Almighty God. If one gloats over the weakness of an enemy, one must also cringe before

85

the power of God. Consciousness of God's all-embracing power leads the victor to forgive his vanquished enemy, despite the latter's helplessness, for the victor knows that in so doing, he is grasping a golden opportunity to win God's forgiveness for himself.

Moses once asked the Lord which of His servants was dearest to Him. The Lord replied: "One who forgives even when he has the power to do otherwise."

Anger

Of all the human emotions, the most destructive is anger. It tears apart human relationships, shatters the harmony of the environment and destablizes whole communities. It must be recognized as one of the worst negative forces in society, and, as such, be kept under strict control.

Alas, it is an emotion which affects all human beings at some time or another, and keeping it under tight rein is often a matter of the greatest difficulty. Fury can be so blinding that it causes a man to forget all norms of human decency—to the point of wishing to humiliate, injure or even kill an opponent. He descends to using vile, harsh language, even comes to blows, all in the attempt to beat his opponent either verbally or physically. His anger does not allow him to see that in so doing he degrades himself as much as the object of his rage. And it is not just the weak, the egoistic, or the ill-natured who fall a prey to such baneful impulses, but even the most morally upright and socially irreproachable members of the community.

Anger gives a momentary illusion of strength, but in actual fact it weakens, degrades and destroys. An otherwise excellent character is seriously marred by fits of rage, for that is what causes a man to forget all his moral precepts and throw his principles to the winds. It was not without good reason that the Prophet said, "A strong man is not one who overwhelms his opponent. A strong man is one who controls himself when he becomes angry."

The advice which the Prophet gave to his companions is advice which we need to follow today: "When one of you becomes angry, he should keep quiet."

But, truly, there is only one thing in this world which can prevent an irate person from going beyond the bounds of decency, and that is *the fear of God*. When an awareness of God's greatness is truly lodged in an individual's heart, this enables him to rein himself in so that he does not stray beyond the limits laid down for him by the Almighty. His consciousness of the fact that God will call him to account for each and every one of his actions exercises a powerful restraint upon the anger surging within him. Such is the character of one who fears God, that when he is made angry by a human being, it is God who looms up before him, effectively quelling his anger.

The Quran makes it clear that any such strong, adverse, emotional reaction such as anger does not befit the true believer, and instead cites as a mark of excellence the quality of forgivingness: "When they become angry, they are forgiving" (42:37). The true believer must cultivate the capacity to rise above negative sentiments in his dealings with people so that his relationships with them remain on a positive basis. When anger and bitterness well up inside him, he should not give vent to these feelings but should, instead, contain and suppress them within his own self. He should live in the world in the way that the flowers do—giving off a sweet fragrance even to those who give nothing but abuse, and remaining unruffled even in the face of violent attack.

After making a mistake

However upright one may be, one cannot help but err from time to time in one's dealings with one's fellow-men. There are bound to be occasions when one fails to give

87

another his due or neglects some responsibility towards him. The Quran tells us that at such times we should right the wrongs we have done by immediately doing good. If we lose no time in doing so, we can effectively cancel out any harmful consequences of our wrong-doing. To this end the Prophet counselled: "Fear God wherever you are, and follow up a bad deed with a good deed. In so doing, you will right whatever wrong you have done." This can take various forms. It can mean asking for forgiveness, praying for the one who has been wronged, giving him a present by way of making amends, speaking well of him to others or generally acting as his well-wisher.

The people of paradise

According to the Quran Paradise will be free of idle talk and sinful speech. There shall be no lying, no false accusations, and no denigration of others. There will be the most sublime feeling of peace and goodwill, for there will be no ridicule, no abuse, in short, no remarks which are even to the slightest degree inappropriate or this to be a reality, it will be only those who are truly superior in character who will be ushered through its portals. Paradise is no place for the low in character. It is a place where only the noble shall reside.

It is of the greatest importance then to build up a good character while still in this world, for it is only those who are possessed of the highest qualities of character who will be eligible to take up their abode in Paradise. Those who fall below this high standard will be discarded like so much rubbish and cast into the pit of Hell, there to suffer eternal punishment for the wickedness of their ways.

8

Islamic Society

The God sought out by one believer is that very same God sought out by other believers. Just as one believer's life is governed by what he imagines his fate will be in the Hereafter, so are the lives of other believers lived out according to the same principles. This being so, how is it at all possible for one believer to come into conflict with another? It is an unfortunate fact that good has been pitted against evil in the world — and every believer knows this full well — for the companions of Satan are free to act in whatever manner they choose. It is essential then, that when the forces of evil have to be contended with, all Muslims should remain united. In so doing, they will increase their strength many times over, thus enabling themselves the more successfully to fight the forces of evil that bar their progress towards their Lord.

One of the most important aspects of living together in a society is the quality of the relationships which develop between its different members. Love, tenderness, care, affection, friendliness and consideration should mark every relationship — be it that of relative, neighbour, friend, vendor, customer, businessman, client, landlord or tenant — to state the position very broadly. But, all too often, bonds once formed in love and friendship are marred, or even broken, by hate, callousness, hostility, indifference, cunning, greed, envy, if not downright criminality. In living side by side with one another, and in serving each others needs, society's members are constantly obliged to have dealings with one another, and it is in the matter of these everyday transactions that all kinds of issues arise which can call forth a negative human reaction. But this is only in the nature of things, for unlike stones, lying unmoved and unmoving, all together in a heap, human beings rub shoulders with each other, and that is when the sparks fly! That is when a streak comes to the surface which pushes them further and further into contentiousness, whereas what is needed is self-restraint and refusal to enter into conflict. Greed, opportunism and the desire to dominate are to blame for much of the friction in society, while on the other side of the coin, there is over-sensitivity, inertia and ignorance. In the face of such human frailty, how can social relationships be expected to retain their positive qualities? How are they to withstand disagreement, strife and friction? Will they not be constantly impaired, if not actually destroyed, by such negative human activity?

As far as Muslims are concerned, they are not left in any doubt as to how they should conduct themselves in their social living, for they are given clear injunctions on this subject in the chapter in the Quran entitled, The Chambers. This enjoins believers to live together as brothers, and to be as quick to settle any quarrels which may break out between them as they would be to put out a fire which had broken out in their own hearth and home. Great stress, in fact, is laid on the avoidance of all such evils as are likely to mar human relationships. One such evil is the heaping of scorn on those who seem sadly lacking in some respects. It is advised never to do this, because those who strike us as being deficient in so many ways may be the very people who are highest in the esteem of their Creator. Who are we to ridicule and sit in judgement? The only true judge of men is God Almighty Himself. It is likewise strictly against the rules laid down in the Quran to misrepresent another and then destroy his reputation. So is pronouncing

90

someone guilty on the basis of suspicion or hearsay, without sufficient evidence to prove his guilt. Delving into the secrets of others is also disallowed, for this can be extremely embarrassing if not downright injurious. Imagine how we ourselves would feel if all our secrets were exposed. Should we not, therefore, wish the same for others as we wish for ourselves? Then the making of damaging remarks about another, when he is not there to defend himself, is deemed a cowardly act of injustice, and, as such, to be eschewed at all costs.

The only way in which these social ills may be eradicated is for people to live in fear of God. It is only if they are ever conscious that God is watching over them, and will call them to account for all their actions in the Hereafter, that they will acquire the qualities that make for a good, healthy society. Their state of awareness will act as a rein on any excesses they may feel inclined to commit, and will restrain them from doing any injustice to their fellow men.

Here are a few sayings of the Prophet which throw some light on the teachings of Islam on particular aspects of social living:

"One is not a true believer until one wishes for one's brother what one wishes for oneself."

"There are three things belonging to a Muslim, which for all Muslims should remain inviolate: his blood, his property and his honour."

"A Muslim is one from whose tongue and hand other Muslims are safe."

"The believers, in their warmth, consideration and compassion for one another, should be like a single body. When there is a complaint in one limb of the body, then the whole body is aroused, and the fever felt throughout it."

"A Muslim is a brother to another Muslim: he neither oppresses his brother, nor does he leave him in the lurch. Whoever helps his brother can count on the help of God, and whoever removes some hardship for a Muslim, will be relieved by God of some hardship on the Day of Resurrection, while one who keeps a Muslim's secrets will have his secrets kept by God on that Day."

"Almighty God has told me to be humble: one person should not commit excesses against another, nor should one look down on anyone."

"A Muslim is to another Muslim as one part of a building is to another part: each part strengthens the other parts." Here the Prophet interlaced his fingers to illustrate this.

The picture of Islamic Society which emerges from these sayings of the Prophet shows how a believer should live amongst his fellows: he should look upon them not as strangers, but as if they were a part of himself. When the conduct of others makes him happy, he should realize from this what will make others happy, and act accordingly. Conversely, when he feels distressed by the behaviour of others, he should realize how troubled others would be if he served them in like manner. He is, therefore, careful not to treat anyone in this way. The feeling for one another in any Muslim community should be so great that the whole social framework becomes like one single body. That is, when pain is felt in one part of the body, the rest of the body should immediately register it. In this way, the distress of one single Muslim would quickly extend to other Muslims who would not then be at peace with themselves until they had relieved their brother of his pain.

The nature of Islamic society must be such that day-to-day dealings are marked with mutual kindness, esteem and consideration. People should be as ready to assist each other in times of need as they would be to take action in the case of their own need. For example, when one sees another homeless and destitute, one should feel as if it were oneself, and not another, who lacked a home and the basic necessities of life; with this feeling in one's heart, one could not then just leave one's brother in the lurch. Then, as to the manner in which one embarks on a suitable course of action, all one's deeds should be carried out in a spirit of humility, and with the idea of doing justice to all. There could be no question then of behaving with arrogance, attempting to assert one's superiority, or even of feeling jealous of anyone who excelled in some particular way. Everyone should wish his fellows well, and be like a close companion to them all the days of his life.

If this could be the general attitude, no one would ever think it permissible to shed so much as a drop of another Muslim's blood, no matter how great the wrong he had suffered at his hands. As for laying hands on another Muslim's property, this would be sedulously avoided. In this way Muslim honour would remain inviolate, for each would guard the honour of his neighbour as if it were his very own.

A society in which everyone is just in his behaviour towards others, and unfailingly wishes others well, is bound to be one of exceptional unity. The more pervasive the atmosphere of mutual goodwill, the higher the degree of unification. If we think of the members of a Muslim society as being the bricks which make up a massive building, we see how each separate brick, being inextricably linked to the other bricks, gives strength to those others and to the entire building. Each brick may be a separate entity, but the connection between it and the others — always close and never in conflict — is one of interdependence and harmony. It is the function of the brick, not to destabilize the edifice, but to consolidate it. It does not seek to fashion the building after its own style, but rather moulds itself to whatever shape will produce a strong and durable structure.

What is required for such an Islamic society to come into being? The answer is simply that people should fear God. The secret of all good in this world is the fear of God, while the absence of this fear is the root of all evil. The companions of the Prophet used to observe that "your greatest well-wisher is one who fears God with regard to you." Indeed, it is the truly God-fearing man who is predisposed to treat others well.

There can be no better rein upon an individual's actions than the thought that God will one day call him to account for his deeds. When one is on the point of being overwhelmed by some animal instinct, or one feels tempted to assert oneself at the expense of others in some matter of honour, prestige or vested interests, there is only one thing which can keep such urges in check so that one does not deviate from the path of justice, and that is the clear realisation that all matters will be judged by God and that no one will ever escape punishment for his misdeeds. One might conceivably escape being punished in this world, but there is absolutely no way that one will be able to escape God's punishment in the world beyond the grave.

A Muslim society should be one of mutual benevolence and justice for all, but this can only be so if all its members have the fear of God in their hearts. When one Muslim has dealings with another, he should not feel that he has to do with a mere human being, but that it is God Himself — God with every strength at his command — with whom he has to deal. Every human being should strike him as a creature sustained by his Maker, and he should never forget that every thing he does in life will finally be judged by God, who has full knowledge of both his inner thoughts and his outward deeds. A Muslim should bear it ever in mind that one day he will die, and shall have to give an account of himself to God. He keeps praying to God to be kind and compassionate towards him on the Day of Judgement. This very prostration of himself before God will make him kindhearted and compassionate towards his fellowmen. He will forgive others for the excesses they commit against him, hoping that in this way he will earn God's forgiveness for his own excesses. He will be generous to others in the hope

94

that God will be generous to him. He will give to others more than he receives from them, for he hopes that, in return for even the most paltry of his good deeds, great rewards will be bestowed upon him by God.

In an Islamic society, the individual should be more conscious of his responsibilities than of his rights; when there is cause for disagreement, or he has a grudge against someone, he should be ready to acknowledge his own errors whenever he himself is in the wrong. Abu Hurayrah tells of how one of the Prophet's creditors, a Bedouin, demanded repayment of his debt in the most uncouth manner. The Prophet's companions, who happened to be present at the time, took offence at the way the man had expressed himself and made to strike him. But the Prophet restrained them, saying, "Leave him alone, for one who is in the right can say whatever he pleases." Thus, taking the blame for the Bedouin's behaviour upon his own shoulder, he set the correct example: that one who is in the right should be allowed to demand his dues. Were this fine example to be followed, all kinds of evils would be eradicated from society.

A definite characteristic of a truly Islamic society is the extreme degree of consideration which its members show for one another. The Prophet's wife Aishah tells of how the Prophet said: "God is gentle: He favours gentleness in all matters." Another tradition related by Abu Hurayrah describes how a desert Arab came to Medina one day and proceeded to relieve himself in the Prophet's mosque. Members of the congregation ran to seize him and give him a sound thrashing, but, when the Prophet saw what was happening, he called them back and told them to leave him alone. "Throw a vessel of water over the place where he has urinated. You have been sent to make things easy for people, and not to make things more difficult."

It is true that an Islamic society is one of very strict

principles, but it is one which is also marked by people's kindness and consideration towards others, one sign of a true believer being his strictness with himself, and his tolerance towards others.

To bear out the principles of Islam, the emphasis should be more on actions than on words. Anas, a companion of the Prophet, tells of a Muslim who died waging a holy war. Someone commented that he could rejoice in the knowledge that he would go to Paradise. But the Prophet disagreed: "How can you tell? It may be that this man engaged in futile talk, and indulged in unworthy miserliness." On another, similar occasion, the Prophet said: "God does not look at how you appear, but at your actual deeds." An Islamic society should, therefore, be a serious-minded society, in which its members should refrain from idle chatter and apply themselves diligently to the more important of life's tasks.

Another characteristic of a truly Islamic society is that its members work for their living. They do not make demands, but earn whatever they receive. They never think of snatching things away from others, but use their God-given faculties to provide themselves with the necessities of life. Abu Abd al-Rahman Auf ibn Malik recounts how one day when there were about nine of the Prophet's companions with him, he had a conversation with them which set their feet on the right course of hard work and independence: "Are you not going to swear allegiance to the Prophet of God?" Since they had already sworn their allegiance not so very long beforehand, they replied: "We have just sworn allegiance, O Messenger of God." But the Prophet said to them again: 'Are you not going to swear allegiance to the Prophet of God?" So they all extended their hands and said: "We swear allegiance at your hand, O Messenger of God. What is that oath that we must swear?" the Prophet replied, "That you will worship God, not associating any partner with him: that you will pray five times a day and follow God's commandments," then the Prophet added: "And do not ask anything of men." Struck by the earnestness of these words, some of those present on this occasion became so scrupulous in following the Prophet's advice, that they would take the trouble to dismount from the horses to pick up a whip which they had let fall to the ground, rather than ask anyone to pick it up for them. This simply means that in an Islamic society the prevailing atmosphere is not one in which people beg and make demands on one another. It is one in which there is emphasis on working for a living and not looking to others for the fulfillment of one's needs.

Abu Qatadah, one of the Prophet's Companions, tells of how the Prophet stood up in their midst and said: "Struggle for God's cause and faith in Him are the most excellent of actions." One of his listeners stood up and asked: "O Messenger of God! If I am slain in God's path, will my sins be forgiven?" The Prophet assured him that they would, if he was slain in the path of God, provided that he had remained steadfast and fought solely for the sake of God, and that he had been pressing forward and not retreating. After some time, the Prophet asked the questioner to repeat his question. When he had done so, the Prophet gave him the same answer, but added that if he were in debt to anyone, this debt would not be forgiven, "for this is what the angel Gabriel has told me."

This shows how careful everyone in an Islamic society must be, neither to appropriate anything which is due to another, nor to trample on another's rights. A Muslim should bear in mind that however great his sacrifices in the path of God have been, these will have value in the eyes of God only if he can go to meet his Lord without having denied others their rights, or refused their legitimate demands, for, even if he gives his very life in God's cause, this will not save him in the life after death, if he has been

97

deficient in these respects.

When the Prophet once exhorted people to give alms, one of his listeners asked: "What if one has nothing to give?" To this the Prophet replied: "Then speak to people kindly, for that is also a form of charity." "And what if one has no kind words to offer?" the man asked. The Prophet then said: "Then avoid inflicting evil on others." What this implies is that the best person in an Islamic society is the one who does most good to others. He is one who gives to others from that which he has been given by God. He benefits others in both word and action. The least that one can do in this respect is to avoid inflicting harm on others. If one is not able to give, at least one should not take away. If one cannot help another, one should at least not make things more difficult for him. Should one have no gentle words to offer, one should avoid hurting others with words of bitterness and wrath.

In his *Muwatta*, Imam Malik writes that a man once came to the Prophet and asked him to give him some words of guidance on which he could base his life. The Prophet told him quite simply to avoid becoming angry. A truly Islamic society consists of people who are fully conscious of the negative effects of anger, and who, therefore, sedulously suppress all such feelings. In this way, they are able to keep themselves in such a positive frame of mind that they can face provocation without stooping to anger, hate, vengeance, envy or scorn. They are able, on the contrary to follow the path of love, justice, benevolence, forgiveness, and magnanimity.

Whenever any issue arises which could be the cause of friction, one should think about it coolly and decide upon that course of action which is most in accord with the will of God. Impulsive action should be avoided and there should be no question of revenge. On the contrary, one should never lose sight of the fact that one is going to have to answer to the Almighty for one's actions. It does not befit a

Muslim to nurse sentiments of anger, hate and vengeance; his life should rather be governed by an attitude of tolerance and forgiveness. He should make a point of never succumbing to anger and should give no place in his life to feelings of vengeance and hatred.

In an Islamic society, when one person does justice to another and gives another his rightful due, this is more than a purely moral or humanitarian act on his part. It is a kind of investment for the life after death, for it is upon his conduct in situations where ethics are all-important that his eternal fate depends: only one who treats others well can expect good treatment for himself at the hands of God. One who fails to treat his fellow human beings in a decent fashion will have no share of God's everlasting blessings in the world to come.

It is in one's treatment of others that man is being tested in this world, and this is of special importance in the case of weak and helpless souls, for when one treats such people in a decent manner, it is for the sake of God, there being no other incentive in this case. But when one treats a powerful person well, it is partly in the hopes that one will receive something in return. Similarly if one takes a humanitarian stance when popular passions have been aroused, one's motivation is determined to a great extent by the anticipation of the fame and prestige which will ensue.

The case is very different when a human being —alone and powerless—stands before one and appeals for help. Here there is no inducement to be helpful, and if one bears some grudge against this powerless supplicant, the urge to help is considerably diminished. Anyone who comes to the aid of such a person, therefore, shows himself to be a selfless and forgiving human being. He is acting thus solely for the sake of God, for in this instance, apart form the Almighty's pleasure, there is nothing further to be gained.

It is one who shows kindness to others, purely for the sake of God, who is the dearest of all God's servants. When he soothes the pain of one of God's servants—doing so only for the sake of God—at that very moment he finds God Himself.

9

Organisation

Within even the tiniest of seeds, God has concealed the beginning of a verdant plant: from one tiny kernel can spring forth the loftiest of trees. But this potentiality can be realized only when all of the condition for its growth are just right—the season, the soil, the temperatures, the sunshine, the rainfall, all must be exactly what the plant needs and only then will our seed sprout and produce the most wonderful of foliage, blossoms and fruits. Suppose we just dropped our seed on a table top and left it to its own resources, there would be no question of its producing a plant, green or otherwise.

Why should this be so? It is because God has created the correct combination of conditions for growth to take place, and has laid down a definite pattern for the functioning of every single thing and every single living creature on this earth. This divine pattern has been ordained for all time, and there is nothing which can exist without conforming to it. The slightest deviation from this pattern produces bad results, or no results at all, whereas acting in accordance with it causes all of God's creations to thrive and flourish.

The same is true of our human communities. Once they are entrusted with the divine code of life, as enshrined in the Book of God, they need only adhere strictly to it, never deviating from the "right path", as it is termed in the Quran, to be able to take root and flourish both in this world and the Hereafter.

The right path is that of adherence to a certain discipline in life according to which human beings should live as though bound by a contract made with God. The right path, in fact, will lead man straight to God.

It is written in the Quran:

> God made a covenant with the Children of Israel and raised among them twelve chieftains. He said: 'I shall be with you. If you attend to your prayers and pay the poor-due; if you believe in My apostles and assist them and give God a goodly loan, I shall forgive you your sins and admit you to gardens watered by running streams. But he that hereafter denies me shall stray from the right path' (5:12).

This contract—or covenant—stipulates several religious duties, the first of which is prayer, a way of bowing to God and seeking to be close to Him. Next is *zakat* which obliges one to be good in giving to others, to behave, in fact, as if they had a basic right to a share in one's earnings. Then there is the duty to spread the word of God. When one hears the call of truth one is obliged to commit oneself unstintingly to its support and furtherance, and to give one's whole-hearted assistance to those who call mankind to the truth. All of these religious duties taken together are what make up the contract according to which a Muslim must pattern his life. Those who live their lives in such a manner find themselves close to God, and become worthy of His divine assistance.

In order to preserve this God-fearing aspect of life in its true form, Muslims have been called upon to organize themselves, i.e. to set up a system in their society based upon what the Quran calls "hearing and obeying". For this system to function effectively, it must be supervised by community leaders who, once appointed, have to be obeyed irrespective of personal likes or dislikes. Religious duties, such as regular attendance at prayers, broad-scale collection and distribution of *zakat,* the systematic propagation of the message of true religion can all be the more effectively carried out once a definite social order has been established in each Muslim community, for it provides a framework within which devotees consider it their bounden duty to follow the lead of those appointed to its upkeep.

The task of organizing Muslim brethren need not fall to a governmental body, for this is a duty which ought to be undertaken by the people themselves, irrespective of whether Muslims are in political power or not, and regardless of general circumstances. Such organization is, in itself an act of worship, but its aims will be fulfilled only if it is carried out without any external pressure being exerted on the individuals concerned: it will bear fruit only if people engage in it of their own free will.

From the Islamic viewpoint, the organization of society is symbolic of man's submission to the word of God. Adherence to Islamic social order demonstrates not only man's obedience to God, but his having passed the most crucial test in life. Those who refrain from subjecting themselves to such an order live in defiance of God's commandments, thus failing in life's greatest trial.

Political power, it should be emphasized, does not in itself ensure the effective organization of Islamic society. During the respective Caliphates of Uthman and Ali, the Muslims wielded political power, yet their organization had become disoriented. Latter-day Islamic history abounds in comparable examples. A social order, to be truly Islamic, must evince itself in a spontaneous system or organization. Such as we see in a mosque, with an Imam leading the faithful in the offering of their daily congregational prayers. Although this entails the restriction of personal freedom for the sake of God, one's submission to such a system must be purely voluntary.

Indeed, an individual who subjects himself to an Islamic social order will be deemed worthy of divine reward only if he does so of his own free will. Organization which has been imposed upon people may yield certain worldly gains, but it cannot in any religious sense benefit those who have undergone coercion. Nor will such organization itself receive God's blessings, for that is reserved for such systems as have been established in a truly Islamic spirit.

A good example of such organization is to be found in the time of the Prophet, prior to the Muslims' emigration to Medina, and, of course, before an Islamic government had been established there. When seventy three men came from Medina to Mecca to swear their allegiance to the Prophet, the latter introduced a system of organization into their ranks by instructing them to elect twelve people from amongst themselves, who would then be responsible for conducting their affairs.

When the Muslims left Arabia, spreading out to various other lands, they formed organizations of this nature wherever they went, and lived ordered lives within this framework. So long as this lasted, they lived into the shade of divine protection. It was only when they deliberately rejected such organization and the discipline it entails that they found themselves bereft of God's protection. Despite their continuing to hold political power, they were eventually subjugated by other nations.

Those who enter this Islamic form of organization quite voluntarily–as required by Islam– give definite proof in doing so of their total selflessness. In this way, they show their capacity to suppress their own egos for the greater glory of God. And, indeed, there is no greater act of piety that one can perform. Those who show themselves ready to make such a sacrifice will have multiple blessings bestowed on them by the Almighty, and in this world, they will be granted honour and supremacy. In the Hereafter their status will be far above that of the egoists and self-seekers.

When those who have been completely subservient to God — to the point of becoming selfless souls — are confronted with the truth, they never hesitate to acknowledge it to be so. Nor do they ever launch themselves on any course of action which might prove ruinous to themselves or to others, either in this world or in the next, for they are prevented from doing so by that very selflessness which makes them bow to God. Never indeed, would they be found to forsake the path of justice.

In truth, all goodness, both in this life and in the Hereafter, lies in selflessness; an individual's selflessness, or his lack of it, can be seen in his response to organization. The binding of oneself to an organized life can be achieved only by those who have raised themselves above the level of selfish motivation. One who has attained this superior moral status becomes indifferent to praise or blame, and, conversely, his opinion of others does not depend upon whether they agree or disagree with him. Personal likes or dislikes are in no way permitted to mould his behaviour. And whether he has been given his due or not, makes not the slightest difference to him, for, ethically, he is a self-sufficient being.

In the course of a religiously organized life, one has continual opportunities of proving one's mettle in these respects. But if mundane concerns have come in the way of accepting the discipline of such an organized life, one will remain perpetually enslaved by the dictates of one's own ego, and will lose the opportunity to develop one's moral potential.

Those who believe in God, and subject themselves to Islamic discipline, can expect to have countless blessing bestowed upon them. Two of these stand out from the others in importance. The first enables a man to become deserving of divine succour, thus placing him in a position to overcome his opponents with the help of the Almighty, while the second saves him from hell-fire in the Afterlife, thus clearing the way for him to be admitted to the Gardens of Paradise. These blessings are reserved for those and those alone who have suppressed the 'self' for the sake of God, having bound themselves to a social order according to which all their religious and ethical activities are properly organized.

The greatest strength of any society is its unity, and what is most damaging to that unity is the relentless pursuit or personal ambition on the part of its members. It is only when people surrender their individuality to God — to the point of becoming totally absorbed in His Being — that they put an end to this pursuit. It is the society made up of such individuals that speaks with one voice and acts as one body. Where such unity exists, there can be no question of defeat.

Before the advent of Islam, tribalism prevailed in Arabia, each tribe living separately from the other. Barbaric customs were practised and the tribes were usually at war with one another. However, when the Prophet brought God's message to them, they entered the fold of Islam, thus effectively terminating internecine warfare. From then onwards, they lived together as brothers. How could such a change have come about? The answer is to be found in the change of attitude engendered by their acceptance of Islam. Without Islam, a man owes allegiance to no one but himself, whereas, with Islam, a man forgets himself and owes allegiance to none but the Almighty. A whole society made up of truly Islamic individuals is consequently able to banish the confusion and disunity arising out of divided loyalties.

It is in owing allegiance to God alone that a people is blessed with unity. It is in bowing to Him that they are imbued with a true sense of direction and purpose, and that their society will advance as if all its members were bound by one and the same rope. From such a society the causes of controversy and disunity will automatically vanish.

The lives of those who adopt religion on the level of in-

106

dividual sacrifice become truly oriented towards God. They proceed unswervingly along a path which will bring them close to the Almighty and to everlasting life with Him. They can never lose their way, and will never let themselves slip from that straight and narrow path, for it is their deepest conviction that it will take them straight to God, and to the Garden which He has prepared for them.

10

The Universality of Islam

Islam dates back to the year 610 AD. At that time there lived in the Arabian town of Yathrib (later known as Medina) two tribes – the Aws and the Khazraj – who were constantly at war with each other. However, when they became aware of the truth of the religion revealed to the Prophet Mohammed, and entered the fold of Islam, they stopped fighting altogether, and these once deadly enemies now became close allies. Formerly the lust for gain had led these tribes to adopt a warlike stance towards each other, but now, imbued with higher ideals, they joined hands with each other in the quest for human progress.

How was it that such a great change came about in the attitude of these two tribes? The reason is that, prior to the advent of Islam, they had thought only of their own greatness. The Aws were bent on asserting their supremacy over the Khazraj, and vice versa. This inevitably led to conflict between the two tribes, with no prospect of their ever being reconciled to each other, or living together in harmony. Now, having one common object of worship which they could both revere, their concept of individual greatness merged into a shared consciousness of the greatness of One God. This, more than anything else, is the source of the spirit of universal brotherhood which Islam gives to the world.

It is in teaching the oneness of God, that Islam teaches the brotherhood of man. This one God of Islam created the world, and He it is who sustains it and controls its affairs. Everything man owns is a gift from God. If God chooses to withhold His bounty, there is no other being who can give it. God is infinite, while all other things are finite. This is the concept which makes of Islam both a monotheistic and a universal religion.

When a man fully accepts *tawheed* (monotheism) as his creed, he cannot but attribute all greatness to God Almighty. All other creatures then become lesser beings in his sight, and the hierarchies and forms of discrimination which exist in society appear to him in their true colours, as things of man's own making. The distinctions which have been set up amongst men on the basis of caste, creed, colour, race or nationality become meaningless to him, for all human beings take on the same humble status as servants of God, owing their allegiance to one Lord and Master.

Before a man has discovered God, he views human beings in relation to himself, and to one another. This superficial way of looking at human affairs leads to a discriminatory attitude which takes account of who are weak and who are strong, who are rich and who are poor, who are great and who are lowly. These distinctions are no doubt valid when one views human beings in relation to one another, but they disappear altogether when one views human beings in relation to their Maker; no man is great, strong or wealthy when compared to God Almighty.

God is the Maker and Master of the entire universe. In comparison to Him, the strong and the weak are all the same, for, before Him, no one possesses any strength. So great is the power of God that all human power dwindles to nothing before His might. It is like the light of a lantern which appears quite radiant in pitch darkness, but which appears to give forth no light at all when the sun rises. Even a searchlight, which is of blazing intensity in the dark, is reduced to the dimmest of rays before the majesty of the sun. There is, in fact, no difference between the lantern and the searchlight after the sun has risen.

Just as the dawn opens man's mind to a new and more powerful source of light, so does *tawheed* broaden the individual's vision to the point of seeing all human beings in one light. When God appears in all His might, human strength in comparison pales into insignificance.

For believers, He becomes the sole focus of human endeavour, and this gives them a sense of human equality, for just as one man strives to please God, so does his neighbour work towards the same goal. Just as one man gives up all claims to greatness for the sake of God, so do all men do so in equal measure. Without *tawheed,* people set their sights on separate goals. With *tawheed,* all men have a superior goal for which to strive. There can be no greater unifying factor than this. It is *tawheed* and *tawheed* alone which will bring about the oneness of mankind.

For thousands of years prior to the advent of Islam, the Arab people had inhabited the Arabian peninsula, yet, in all that long period, had accomplished nothing worth recording in history. They were noted only for their poetry, and for their readiness to go to war with one another over trivial issues. Sometimes when such fighting broke out, it would continue from generation to generation.

However, when they came under the influence of Islam, such a revolution took place in their thinking that these same feuding Arabs, who had no livelihood outside their own limited sphere, were able to lay the foundation of a great world civilization. Spreading far beyond their former geographical boundaries, they dispersed among the countries of the globe. A people, who had previously been dismissed as intellectually negligible, progressed beyond all other nations in every contemporary field of knowledge. The Arabic language, which had enjoyed no greater status than that of a local dialect, was transformed into an international language. Those who had previously been members of a closed society, became masters of a great new world.

The reason for this transformation was the universal nature of Islam. Previously, these people had worshipped the phenomena of nature, but then Islam brought enlightenment to them: it taught them that nature is but a part of God's creation, having no power of its own. Thus, minds which had formerly been closed, were opened up by Islam. People learned from it that only God is worthy of being worshipped; it is God and God alone who has control over all mankind and all creation.

Now instead of seeing nature as an object of worship, the Arabs came to see it as a subject of research. It now became something which could be investigated and made use of. Instead of being served, it could now be harnessed to serve man.

Hitherto, mankind had been divided into different categories: Arabs and Asians, black and white, free men and slaves, the mighty and the lowly. But Islam removed all these dividing lines and set all these distinctions at naught. It impressed upon people that if everyone was subservient to one God, and Adam was the progenitor of all mankind, there could be no difference between one human being and another. This belief kindled a universal spirit which caused people to regard all countries as their own, and to think of every nation as a member of a great world family. Before the coming of Islam, the Arabs had been a race apart, living in seclusion from the rest of the world. But once they had embraced Islam, they were led to mix with other nations and to become their companions and partners on life's journey.

Under the influence of Islam, Arab tribalism, with its straining after short-term gains, and its reverence for some and scorn for others, gave way to the kind of internationalism which had respect for the whole of humanity. The Arabs had their vision so broadened by Islam that they

111

crossed land and sea to give full expression to their new concept of fraternal living. No mountain was too high for them to climb. No ocean was too deep for them to cross.

The Arabs now made advances in every field. In navigation, for instance, they produced men of the calibre of Ahmad ibn Majid. He it was who guided the famous explorer, Vasco da Gama, on his voyage across the oceans at the end of the 15th century to discover a sea-route from Europe to India. Christopher Columbus first conceived of the idea that there was a New World waiting to be discovered after studying the results of the research carried out by Abu Obaydah Muslim al-Balansy, a renowned topographer of his day. It was when Columbus set out to discover that world that he made his discovery of America.

Islamic vision extends not just to the world we know, but to the entire cosmos: Muslims can say with justice that theirs is a truly universal religion. This universality of Islam is no empty theory, for the entire history of Islam supports it as a guiding principle which has been consistently put into practice.

Nowhere have the universal principles on which Islam is founded been better expressed than in the encounter between Rabiy ibn Amir, a Muslim envoy, and the Iranian chieftain, Rustam. During the caliphate of Umar Faruq the Arabs had entered Iran and had proceeded to beat the Iranians in one battle after another, so that a stage had come when Rustam, as commander-in-chief of the Iranian armies, thought it prudent to invite an Islamic delegation to visit his court. When they arrived there to enter into discussions. Rustam, wearing a diamond-studded gold crown, reclined amidst great pomp and splendour on a magnificent throne. The leader of the Islamic delegation, Rabiy ibn Amir, who was humble in bearing and simply clad, presented a striking contrast. When Rustam demanded to know why they had invaded his territory, Rabiy replied quite simply: "God has sent us. We have been brought here

112

by Him so that we may turn away those of His servants whom He wishes from the worship of creation, and bring them to the worship of God; so that we may extract them from the narrow confines of the world and set their feet on its broad, open paths; so that we may save them from the oppression of religions and bring to them the justice of Islam.

This statement by Rabiy, brief as it was, summed up the universal principles on which Islam is based.

When a man's thinking is revolutionized by Islamic teachings, he passes beyond the realms of creation and enters the domain of the Creator. He becomes close to God, who knows no restrictions or limitations. Previously on a human level, he now lives on the level of the divine. Before discovering God, a man is living, as it were, in a cocoon. After discovering God, he makes the vastness of the world his very own.

In normal conditions, people remain immersed— entangled even — in human affairs. Their attention is directed towards creatures like themselves, and they see no further than the ground they walk on. When a man discovers God, however, and devotes his entire life to worshipping Him, he rises far above this mundane, human level. Friendship and enmity mean nothing to him now. The passion of love and the corrosion of jealousy are no longer the mainsprings of his existence. When his soul basks in the vastness of the universe, there can be no further involvement in the petty affairs of this world.

Islam raises one above the hair-splitting arguments which are the hallmark of other religions. It enables one to leave behind all artificial forms of religion, marred as they are by false customs and empty ritual. It acquaints one with true religion, where, on the one hand, stands man, and on the other, his Lord, with nothing whatsoever in between. This is a religion which needs no prop of custom or convention. It is a religion which brings one straight to God without enmeshing one in obscure rites, argumentation and the dubious services of self-styled intermediaries. No such entanglements are necessary in the quest for the Almighty. At every moment, God reaches out to His servants; man may then find God at any moment of his seeking. No barrier stands between man and God, and there is, therefore, no need for intercession. When a man enters the eternal world of God, he finds his Maker right there before him, where he stands.

Islam, the religion of *tawheed* is pure and eternal. The God of Islam is one God: all divinity is invested in His Being. Those who discover the purity of *tawheed* find themselves in an infinite and eternal world, where time and space are limitless, the horizon is without end, and vision knows no boundaries.

Goodword English Publications

The Holy Quran: Text, Translation and Commentary (HB), Tr. Abdullah Yusuf Ali

The Holy Quran (PB), Tr. Abdullah Yusuf Ali

The Holy Quran (Laminated Board), Tr. Abdullah Yusuf Ali

The Holy Quran (HB), Tr. Abdullah Yusuf Ali

Holy Quran (Small Size), Tr. Abdullah Yusuf Ali

The Quran, Tr. T.B. Irving

The Koran, Tr. M.H. Shakir

The Glorious Quran, Tr. M.M. Pickthall

Allah is Known Through Reason, Harun Yahya

The Basic Concepts in the Quran, Harun Yahya

Crude Understanding of Disbelief, Harun Yahya

Darwinism Refuted, Harun Yahya

Death Resurrection Hell, Harun Yahya

Devoted to Allah, Harun Yahya

Eternity Has Already Begun, Harun Yahya

Ever Thought About the Truth?, Harun Yahya

The Mercy of Believers, Harun Yahya

The Miracle in the Ant, Harun Yahya

The Miracle in the Immune System, Harun Yahya

The Miracle of Man's Creation, Harun Yahya

The Miracle of Hormones, Harun Yahya

The Miracle in the Spider, Harun Yahya

The Miracle of Creation in DNA, Harun Yahya

The Miracle of Creation in Plants, Harun Yahya

The Moral Values of the Quran, Harun Yahya

The Nightmare of Disbelief, Harun Yahya

Perfected Faith, Harun Yahya

Quick Grasp of Faith, Harun Yahya

Timelessness and the Reality of Fate, Harun Yahya

In Search of God, Maulana Wahiduddin Khan

Islam and Peace, Maulana Wahiduddin Khan

An Islamic Treasury of Virtues, Maulana Wahiduddin Khan

The Moral Vision, Maulana Wahiduddin Khan

Muhammad: A Prophet for All Humanity, Maulana Wahiduddin Khan

Principles of Islam, Maulana Wahiduddin Khan

Prophet Muhammad : A Simple Guide to His Life, Maulana Wahiduddin Khan

The Quran for All Humanity, Maulana Wahiduddin Khan

The Quran: An Abiding Wonder, Maulana Wahiduddin Khan

Religion and Science, Maulana Wahiduddin Khan

Simple Wisdom (HB), Maulana Wahiduddin Khan

Simple Wisdom (PB), Maulana Wahiduddin Khan

The True Jihad, Maulana Wahiduddin Khan

Tabligh Movement, Maulana Wahiduddin Khan

A Treasury of the Quran, Maulana Wahiduddin Khan

Woman Between Islam and Western Society, Maulana Wahiduddin Khan

Woman in Islamic Shari'ah, Maulana Wahiduddin Khan

The Ideology of Peace, Maulana Wahiduddin Khan

Indian Muslims, Maulana Wahiduddin Khan

Introducing Islam, Maulana Wahiduddin Khan

Islam: Creator of the Modern Age, Maulana Wahiduddin Khan

Islam: The Voice of Human Nature, Maulana Wahiduddin Khan

Islam Rediscovered, Maulana Wahiduddin Khan

Words of the Prophet Muhammad, Maulana Wahiduddin Khan

God Arises, Maulana Wahiduddin Khan

The Call of the Qur'an, Maulana Wahiduddin Khan

Building a Strong and Prosperous India and Role of Muslims, Maulana Wahiduddin Khan

Islam As It Is, Maulana Wahiduddin Khan

Sermons of the Prophet Muhammad, Assad Nimer Busool